HILL

PHR

David Bradley
(Lahu, Lisu, Karen & Other Hill Tribes)

Paul Lewis (Akha)
Nerida Jarkey (Mong)
Christopher Court (Mien)

Hill Tribes phrasebook
2nd edition

Published by
Lonely Planet Publications
Head Office: PO Box 617, Hawthorn, Vic 3122, Australia
Branches: 150 Linden Street, Oakland CA 94607, USA
            10a Spring Place, London NW5 3BH, UK
            1 rue du Dahomey, 75011 Paris, France

Printed by
SNP Pte Ltd, Singapore

Cover Illustration
Prêt-à-porter by Chelle Rudelson

Published
January 1999

ISBN 0 86442 635 6

About the Authors

Professor David Bradley teaches linguistics and Burmese at La Trobe University in Melbourne, but spends a lot of time in Thailand, China and other places where Lahu, Akha, Lisu and other such languages are spoken. His PhD was done at the School of Oriental and African Studies in London, but his interest in these groups started even before that, at Columbia University with Professor James Matisoff. He is also the author of the Lonely Planet Burmese Phrasebook, a Lisu dictionary, a book on Lahu dialects, and so on.

Dr Paul W Lewis is a retired missionary now living in California. His career from the 1950s to the 1980s was spent working on education, health and economic development among the Akha and Lahu in Burma and Thailand. He has published an Akha dictionary and a Lahu dictionary among other things.

Dr Christopher Court spent many years in Thailand before he completed his PhD on Mien at the University of California, Berkeley. Since then he has been teaching Thai in various places; he is now at the University of Hawaii at Manoa.

Dr Nerida Jarkey completed her PhD on Mong at the Australian National University, and is now teaching Japanese at the University of Sydney.

From the Author

David Bradley wants to thank the other three authors for their contributions. He is also very pleased to acknowledge the help of many Lahu, Lisu, Bisu, Gong and other friends over the years. Love to Maya, and best wishes to all those interested in these groups. Please feel welcome to contact the authors through Lonely Planet or directly.

From the Publisher

This book was edited by Elizabeth Swan. Peter D'Onghia and Sally Steward proofed it while Fabrice Rocher laid it out and designed the cover. The maps were drawn by Piotr Czajkowski and the illustrations by Ann Jeffree, Penelope Richardson and Tamsin Wilson.

CONTENTS

OTHER GROUPS 151

INDEX 163

INTRODUCTION

Almost everyone in Thailand speaks Thai. However, there are several extremely interesting and frequently visited groups in the north of the country who have their own languages and speak Thai much less well. These groups are sometimes called 'hill tribes' in Thailand. The same groups, speaking the same languages, also live nearby in Myanmar (Burma), Laos, southwestern China and parts of northern Vietnam. In these other countries the general term for these groups is 'national minorities', 'ethnic minorities', or 'ethnic groups'. In Thailand the hill tribes have a population of nearly 800,000 or under 2% of the total; in Laos and Myanmar the minorities are nearly half of the total, about a fifth in Vietnam, and nearly a tenth in China overall, but closer to a third in southwestern provinces such as Yunnan. So there are far more people from these groups outside Thailand than in it; most of those in Thailand have arrived there in the last century or two from China via Laos or Myanmar.

You'll thus find that this book is useful when you want to speak with the same group in Myanmar, Laos, Vietnam or China. There are local differences in speech, just as there are in English or Thai, but they usually don't stop everyday conversation. For more modern topics, these languages borrow new words from the local national language. So words like 'train' or 'airplane' may be borrowed from Thai in Thailand, from Burmese in Myanmar, from Lao in Laos, from Vietnamese in Vietnam, and from Chinese in China. If you know the word for something in the national language where you are, you can try to use it in the middle of a sentence in one of these languages and you'll probably be understood.

This book has sections on the languages of five of the largest such groups. The first three are Lahu, Akha and Lisu, three closely related languages which are more distantly connected with Burmese. The other two languages here are Mong and Mien, formerly known as Meo and Yao. These two languages are fairly close to each other but quite different from the languages around them.

INTRODUCTION

LOCAL NAMES OF THE FIVE LARGEST GROUPS

There is a great deal of diversity in the names used for these five groups. The most usual ones are shown in the table below.

	Thailand	Laos	Myanmar	Vietnam	China
Lahu	Musur	Musur	Muhso	Cosung	Lahu
Akha	Ikaw	Kaw	Kaw	Hanhi	Hani
Lisu	Lisaw		Lishaw		Lisu
Mong	Maew	Maew	Myaung	Hmong	Miao
Mien	Yao	Yao	Yaung	Dao	Yao

Some Mong in Thailand, most Mong in Laos and refugees from Laos in western countries pronounce their own name as Hmong instead. The Vietnamese name written 'Dao' is actually pronounced Zao. There are also other names used for local subgroups within these five groups, especially in China which has the largest number and diversity. There are also some older Chinese names for some of these groups which are now regarded as insulting. Indeed, many of the refugees in western countries regard anything but their own name for themselves as inappropriate.

These five groups account for nearly half the total hill tribe population in Thailand and a much higher proportion in the north of the country. Overall there are about 15 million people worldwide who speak these five languages, including over 300,000 in Thailand and five million elsewhere who speak exactly the dialects given here; most of the other 10 million would understand them because they are the major dialects of each language.

CHINA

In China, the Mong are included in the Miao national minority, which at the 1990 census was the fifth largest such group in China. The Mien are part of the Yao nationality which is the 13th largest national minority in China and includes other groups such as the Bunu and the Lajia. The Akha are part of China's Hani nationality, the 16th in size. The Lisu are 20th in China and the Lahu are 24th. China has 50 other national minorities and the Han Chinese majority.

VIETNAM & LAOS

In Vietnam there are the Kinh or Viet majority and 53 minorities, of which the Mong were eighth in the 1993 census, the Mien were ninth, the Akha/Hanhi were 32nd, and the Lahu/Cosung were 38th. Laos officially lists 46 minority ethnic groups, of which the Mong are fourth largest, the Akha are eighth, the Mien are 17th, and two subgroups of Lahu are 25th and 27th; together these two Lahu subgroups would form the 19th largest such group in Laos. There are no Lisu in Vietnam or Laos.

MYANMAR (BURMA)

Myanmar sometimes quotes 135 as the number of ethnic groups, but there are no reliable census statistics available. The last census was in 1983; this was based on police registration records, and didn't even attempt to count much of the mountainous area where most minority groups live. The Lahu, Akha and Lisu are all substantial groups there, but the Mong and Mien are fewer. Current populations for the five groups are given at the beginning of each chapter.

THAILAND

The other main hill tribe of Thailand is the Karen; divided into two main groups, Sgaw in the north and Pho along the western border. Most of the many Karen in Thailand are long-established residents and speak Thai fairly well; hence their two languages are less necessary for travellers and are only briefly discussed here. The Karen of Myanmar speak a much greater variety of languages. The two largest groups there are the southernmost Pho and Sgaw; there are also a few members of the third largest group in Myanmar, the Kayah (Kayinni, Red Karen) in north-western Mae Hong Son province in Thailand.

Lahu, Akha and Lisu, along with Karen, Burmese and several hundred other languages along both sides of the Himalaya, form the Tibeto-Burman subgroup of the Sino-Tibetan language family. The relationship with Tibetan is a fairly distant one, and that with Chinese (the Sino part of Sino-Tibetan) even more so. Apart from Karen and Chinese, all these languages are similar in structure; for example, they end the sentence with the verb, not its object.

It has been suggested that there's a linguistic relationship between Thai languages, Austronesian languages (Indonesian/Malay, Tagalog, Maori and Hawaiian, to name a few; also most other Pacific languages) and Miao-Yao languages including Mong and Mien. Mong and Mien are structurally similar to Thai; for example, the verb comes before its object.

There are also several tribal groups speaking languages of the Mon-Khmer family in Thailand; some of these, such as the roughly 50,000 Htin of Nan province (who call themselves Mal or Pray, and are locally called Lua by the Northern Thai) and some 10,000 Lavüa of south-western Chiang Mai and southern Mae Hong Son provinces (also called Lua in Northern Thai), are substantial localised groups of limited distribution outside Thailand; others, such as the Khmu in Nan province (12,000) and northern Laos (400,000), Vietnam (50,000) and China (5000) or the very numerous Kui (Suai in Thai; not officially counted as a hill tribe) of north-eastern Thailand and northern Kampuchea, are more numerous in adjacent countries. A variety of tiny groups is also subsumed under the general category of Lua in Northern Thai or Lawa in Central Thai with a total of about 20,000 in Thailand. These include the Gong, who speak a Tibeto-Burman language fairly close to Burmese, in western central Thailand; the Bisu, who speak another Tibeto-Burman language closely related to Lahu, Akha and Lisu, in south-western Chiang Rai province; the Palong near Chiang Mai, who speak a Mon-Khmer language; and several others, mostly with only a couple of hundred speakers left. Nearly all speakers of these smaller and in general more assimilated minorities speak Thai fairly well; many local Thai people are the descendants of these groups. See the chapter on Karen and other hill tribes for more details.

In the last 20 years many Westerners have gone on 'hill tribe treks' in northern Thailand. Just about all of them have to rely on a Thai guide, who most probably won't speak any minority language, for slow and inadequate communication with the locals. There are also a few guides who are members of these groups, and you may want to find one of these. With this phrasebook you can begin to speak directly, and the resulting surprise and joy of these people must almost be seen to be believed. Almost all foreigners who speak these languages are missionaries, so you may be assumed to be one; people in some non-Christian villages may therefore be a bit wary at first.

There are many good books on the hill tribes of Thailand. One particularly useful and beautifully illustrated one, available in several languages, is *Peoples of the Golden Triangle* by Paul & Elaine Lewis (Thames & Hudson, London, 1984) and widely available in Thailand. Some older books, such as *The Hill Tribes of Northern Thailand* by O Gordon Young (Siam Society, Bangkok) are out of date but also have some useful information and pictures.

For books on specific tribes, see each chapter for references. *Proto-Loloish* by David Bradley (Curzon Press, London, 1979) provides a summary of the distribution, culture and linguistic history of the Lahu, Akha, Lisu and related groups, and is available from the author or from the publisher.

None of these books is very suitable for carrying to hill tribe villages, but you'll want to have them if you get seriously interested in one or more of these groups. The Tribal Research Institute on the campus of Chiang Mai University has a good library with all the books mentioned in this phrasebook and many more. There's a large new Hill Tribe Museum on the northern outskirts of Chiangmai which replaces the small museum formerly located on the ground floor of the Tribal Research Institute.

The maps provided here can give you a general idea of village locations in Thailand; each village or cluster of villages is shown. Villages move fairly frequently, so the maps are likely to be partly out of date before long. You would definitely need more exact and detailed information to find villages by yourself. Local Thais whom you pass on the road and local pick-up truck drivers may be able to help sometimes, but they don't always know and may give you wrong information when trying to be helpful. Also, of course, they're likely to speak only Thai. Some areas are particularly sensitive or even dangerous, and you must always enquire carefully before setting out.

When you go to a village, you should take almost everything you expect to need: clothing, medicine, protein foods. Take a torch (flashlight) and batteries for use at night, as electricity is rarely available. Rice and some vegetables can usually be found locally, but you can't count on meat. In the cool season (November to February) it can be cold at night, and this is when village people need all their bedding, so you'll need to take a sleeping bag or blankets. In the wet season (May to October) paths are muddy and slippery, so good footwear is important. As water is often brought from fairly far away, bathing and clothes washing isn't done in the village but rather at or below the water source. You should take your soap, towel and toiletries. Drinking water isn't always safe; drink boiled water or tea where possible, and carry some purified water with you on the way. Most of these groups eat with the right hand or with chopsticks; you may decide to take your own bowl, cup and utensils if this is convenient.

The health risks of life in a minority village aren't as great as the Thai and other majority people believe (and will tell you), but they are real. Tuberculosis and malaria are fairly widespread, and minor digestive system problems are also common. With extreme temperature differences between the night and the day you'll also be susceptible to colds.

Finally, you should always give people something if you eat or spend the night; these groups are all much poorer than the majority groups and cannot manage to feed a constant stream of visitors without help. Appropriate practical gifts include special foods, blankets and clothing, or local money. Many villages have a tiny shop attached to someone's house where you can buy tins of fish, matches, cigarettes and so on, but don't rely on this; it may also be difficult to change large notes. Though there's a tradition of free hospitality, you must not abuse it!

THE LANGUAGES

Each of the five languages presented here is written with the Roman alphabet; examples are given in these writing systems, which some hill tribe people in Thailand can read and which represent the sounds quite accurately. Among the Lahu Christians you often find literate speakers, but less frequently elsewhere. There's another Lisu writing system using capital letters, right side up and upside down, which isn't shown here. Unfortunately each writing system has its own rules, so no general pattern for pronunciation can be given. However, a number of features are present in all these languages, and can be summarised here.

All five languages are tonal, like Thai, Chinese and most other languages of South-East and East Asia; that is, the pitch of the voice must be controlled, as the same combination of consonant and vowel means different things under different pitches. Lahu and Akha indicate these tones with small diacritics after the vowel of each syllable; Lisu, Mong and Mien use a consonant after each vowel to signify the tone. Speaking a tone language is not like singing – you don't need to get exactly the same pitch every time; just control the pitch in a relative way. This is done when saying 'Yes.' versus 'Yes?' or 'Yes!' in English, but in English it carries over the whole sentence, not just one word; here each syllable must be controlled for pitch.

All five languages make a contrast of aspiration for sounds such as 'p', 't' and 'k'. This contrast is automatic and when used in English doesn't make a difference to meaning, but must be maintained in these languages or the wrong word will result. In English the 'p', 't' and 'k' preceded by an 's' as in 'spar', 'star' and 'scar' have no puff of air after the consonant; these are called unaspirated. The 'p', 't' and 'k' in 'par', 'tar' and 'car' have a strong puff of air after the consonant; these are called aspirated. You can most easily feel the puff of air by putting your hand in front of your mouth when you say these words. To get used to controlling this difference, you can start by saying a slight 's' sound before the unaspirated consonants, then gradually leaving it off but not releasing the puff of air afterwards; the aspirated sounds present no difficulty for English speakers. Some other European languages use primarily unaspirated sounds, so speakers of these may need to emphasise the pushing out of air for them.

Each language has relatively simple syllable structure, with few sequences of consonants before the vowel and only one, or in some cases no consonant, possible after it; and every syllable has a tone.

Most of the five languages use some vowels that are unlike those of most European languages; these include sounds like 'u' and 'o' but made with the lips spread at the edges rather than rounded. You can try looking in a mirror and controlling the lips to get the idea: make a rounded 'u' or 'o', then keep saying it but spread the lips by smiling. These spread and rounded sounds are different vowels, and must be kept apart. So too must the spread and rounded sounds like German 'i' and 'ü', 'e' and 'ö' or the similar French 'i' and 'u', 'e' and 'eu', which are also distinct sounds in some of these languages.

Furthermore, in most of the vowels there is no tongue movement during the sound; in English 'a' and 'o' glide off into 'i' and 'u' sounds, and 'u' starts with a 'y' sound, but these movements are not found in the hill tribe languages – just as they are absent from many European languages such as French, Italian, and so on.

Like Thai, Chinese and other surrounding languages, all these languages have grammatical features in common. For example, all adjectives function like verbs, so there's no need for a verb like 'to be' in addition to the adjective in a sentence like 'He is tall'. Another example is that every number must be accompanied by a classifier. The noun being counted determines which classifier, so for example 'one person' comes out as 'person one human-classifier' in Lahu, Akha and Lisu; and as 'one human-classifier person' in Mong and Mien.

In some instances question marks aren't used with the hill tribe languages – this is either because the question is presented in the form of a statement, or to indicate that there's no rise in intonation at the end of the sentence. In general, responses to questions involve simply repeating the verb used, with a negative word before it if the reply is negative.

None of these languages has endings on words to mark gender, case, tense or other categories often attached to words in European languages; instead, the corresponding meanings are expressed, if at all, by separate words.

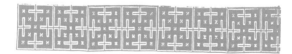

CULTURE, SUBGROUPS & LOCATIONS

The Lahu are a group of over 800,000 people; about 450,000 of these live in relatively remote regions of extreme south-western Yunnan in China, and roughly 250,000 in even more inaccessible parts of north-eastern Myanmar (Burma). There are some 17,000 in Laos, and some refugees from Laos in the USA. There is also a closely related group, the Kucong or Cosung, with about 50,000 people in China and 5000 in Vietnam; these are included in the Lahu 'nationality' there. The approximately 90,000 Lahu in Thailand represent five main subgroups of this complex ethnic group: Black Lahu (La˘hu_na^); Red Lahu (La˘hu_nyi); White Lahu (La˘hu_ hpu); Shehleh (La˘hu_sheh˘ leh-), and Yellow Lahu (La˘hu_shi).

The Lahu have been particularly receptive to new religions. Most of the Black and Yellow Lahu in Thailand are Protestant Christians, the Red Lahu have been following a series of indigenous messiahs from Myanmar for the last 100 years or so, and the White Lahu had their origins in a similar messianic movement in Laos about 50 years ago. Nearly all the Thailand Lahu have come in from Burma, Laos and China over the last century, some as recently as the 1970s.

The Lahu live mainly at fairly high altitudes, though some Christian villages have come down to lower levels in the last 20 years. Villages tend to have a religious centre at or near the top of the village. In the Shehleh villages this is a circular fenced dancing ground and the most interesting time to visit is at the full or new moon, when young people dance and sing there. In the Red and White Lahu villages there is a temple, usually built like a normal Lahu house but sometimes on the ground. In most villages this is *not* open to outsiders so check before you go into a building with wooden pillars inside the fence surrounding it, or with lots of small pennants on high poles around it. In the

Lahu (Musur) in Thailand

LAHU

MYANMAR

LAOS

Chiang Rai

Mae Hong
Song

Phayao

Chiang Mai

Nan

Lamphun

Lampang

Phrae

Uttaradit

Loei

Tak   Sukhotai

Phitsanulok

Phetchabun

Kamphaeng
Phet

Phichit

THAILAND

Nakhon Sawan

Uthai Thani

ANDAMAN
SEA

Suphan Buri

Kanchanaburi

BANGKOK

Ratchaburi

Bight of
Bangkok

Phetchaburi

0   100   200 km

	Yellow
	Red
	Black
	Shehleh
	Other

Christian Black and Yellow Lahu villages the church is usually the most substantial building in the village, and is devotedly used on Sundays. Christians don't work on Sundays, so people tend to be in the village then.

All Lahu celebrate the New Year with special food, music, dancing and singing; in Christian villages this celebration is now done on 1 January. Non-Christians celebrate sometime near Chinese New Year (celebrated in late January or early February), but each village chooses its own New Year celebration date according to work needs so you must check locally. In 1998 this ranged from early January to early March; it lasts four days, with a short break, then another three days. Often people in surrounding villages visit at this time, so accommodation may be scarce.

Traditional Lahu houses are made with wooden house posts, thatched roofs, and everything else bamboo. Floor and roof supports are whole bamboo poles, walls and floors are flattened bamboo slats. The floors are about a metre above ground level, and reached by a ladder or notched log leading up to an uncovered porch. Guests are usually welcomed first on the porch, then may later be invited into the outer room, which contains the hearth and serves as kitchen, meal and storage area, but they normally do not go into the inner sleeping rooms of the family. In non-Christian houses you should avoid the family altar, a small high shelf usually at the very back of the house.

It is quite easy to tell the Lahu subgroups apart, especially by their traditional clothes. The Red Lahu men wear bright green or blue-green baggy Shan-style trousers, rather like the Lisu. The women wear elaborate long shirts open vertically at the front with many horizontal strips of brightly coloured cloth across the chest area. Both wear towels as turbans. The Shehleh women wear distinctive black clothes: black trousers and long black coats with wide white stripes at the edges, while the men wear clothes similar to Red Lahu men. In the last 10 years the colour of the women's clothes has changed; some now use blue or green in-

LAHU

stead of black cloth, and multiple narrow stripes alternating with wider bands of red at the ends of their sleeves. 'Traditional' White Lahu clothes, hardly ever seen now, are white trousers and shirt worn by male priests. The Black and Yellow Lahu wear traditional clothes only at times of celebration, if at all, and indeed many other Lahu now wear non-traditional clothes most of the time.

The most interesting handicrafts of the Lahu are their shoulder bags, which also come in smaller purse-like sizes; belt straps and other items of clothing are also widely available. Less durable are musical instruments, including the gourd reed-organ and the jew's-harp (which is rather hard to play) as well as some Chinese-derived stringed instruments.

All of the few White Lahu in Thailand are in the eastern part of Chiang Rai province; some of these villages are not very welcoming, and most are fairly near the border with Laos and thus not recommended. The Shehleh are scattered in Chiang Mai, Mae Hong Son

LAHU

and Tak provinces, with some very easily accessible and friendly villages near the new road from Chiang Mai to Chiang Rai and some others astride the road from Tak to Mae Sot on the Myanmar border. There are various Christian Black Lahu villages in Chiang Mai and Chiang Rai provinces, notably west of the road from Chiang Mai to Fang, along the upper Kok River and elsewhere. The Christian Yellow Lahu villages are mainly around Chiang Rai and along the lower Kok River, also extending to the south around Mae Sruai and some newer settlements in Kampaengphet and Nakhon Sawan provinces. Christian Lahu are hard-working people and may be less hospitable to visitors than other Lahu. They do not produce or use opium. By far the largest group of Lahu in Thailand is the Red Lahu, found in most parts of northern Chiang Mai, north-western Chiang Rai and northern Mae Hong Son provinces. Within the Red group there are some minor subgroups, such as a couple of Laba villages near the top of the road to Doi Tung; a couple of villages west of Mae Chan, originally mainly Bakeo Yellow Lahu but now mainly Red; and some mixed Red Lahu-Lisu villages along the middle Kok River.

Many traditional Lahu religious texts have been collected by Anthony Walker and published in various places including the *Journal of the Siam Society*. For an overview of the subgroups and dialects of Lahu, see *Lahu Dialects* by David Bradley (Australian National University Press, 1979), available from David Bradley at the Department of Linguistics, La Trobe University, Bundoora Victoria 3083, Australia.

SOUNDS

The sounds of Lahu are consistently represented by the writing system as used here; many Christian Lahu can read and write, but very few non-Christian Lahu are literate. Most of the letters have values which make sense to speakers of languages which use Roman script, as the writing was devised in cooperation with English speakers and uses the Roman alphabet.

LAHU

Vowels

There are only 10 vowels: i, e, eh, u, o, aw, ui, eu, a and uh. The first three are like the vowel sounds in English 'beat', 'bit' and 'bet'; the next three are like 'boot', 'put' and 'bought', though Lahu e and o are said just as long as the other vowels, unlike English 'bit' and 'put'. Of the remaining vowels, a presents no problems; it is like the 'a' of 'father', not like the 'a' of 'fat'.

The vowel ui is similar to the New Zealand or South African pronunciation of the vowel in 'bit', or the second vowel in words such as 'roses'. For eu the closest comparison is the English vowel in 'but' or British English 'fur'. The Lahu vowel uh occurs only after certain consonants and represents a problem in the spelling of Lahu; it sounds like a prolonged 'z' instead of a vowel after s, z, tc, ts, tz, and like a prolonged 'v' or similar sound after pf, hpf, bv and mv. All these vowels are single sounds, not sequences as the two-letter spellings might suggest.

Consonants

One contrast which may be hard for many is the difference between pairs of sounds such as p and hp, t and ht, tc and ts, c and ch, k and hk, k' and hk'. The first of each is unaspirated, while the second has a strong puff of air (aspirated); most of the latter contain an h in the writing, apart from ts which is like a puffed 'ts' sound, contrasting with the puffless 'ts' represented by tc. Also note that c is the puffless version of ch which is similar to English 'ch' as in 'church'; c is not a k-like sound. For more information on aspirated and unaspirated sounds, see the Introduction, page 15.

The sounds represented by k' and hk' are made like the English 'k' in 'coat' or 'cot', that is with a further back 'k' sound; while those represented by k and hk are similar to the English 'k' in 'key' or 'kit', with a further forward 'k' sound; these two contrast in most Lahu dialects (but not Yellow Lahu), as in words such as hkaw^, 'six' versus hk'aw^, 'year', or hka^, 'crossbow' versus hk'a^, 'village'. Unlike these, the sound represented by g' is a sound similar to a throaty growl or a French 'r': not a plain 'g' but rather one made with friction. The other consonants do not present many problems for English speakers.

Tones

The most complex thing about the sounds of Lahu is the tones; there are seven. Actually many Lahu have trouble keeping two of these seven (low falling and low level) apart, and the Shehleh have collapsed two others (high falling and low falling) completely in their speech; but they are absolutely essential to speaking and understanding Lahu. Tones mainly involve the pitch of the voice; it's not quite like singing, but you must control the pitch for each syllable.

The tones are:

high falling	indicated by a raised ˘ after the vowel
mid level	indicated by the absence of any mark
low falling	indicated by a lowered ˬ after the vowel
low level	indicated by an underline _ after the vowel
high rising	indicated by ¯ after the vowel
high short	indicated by ^ after the vowel
low short	indicated by lowered ‸ after the vowel

For example:

ca˘	eat
ca	look for
caˬ shi_	rice grain
ca_	feed
ca¯	join
ca^	a strip
ca‸	push

Don't ignore these tones, as they make a difference to the meaning, as in Thai and most other languages of the area. The tones of Yellow Lahu are quite different, but as noted above most Yellow Lahu in Thailand can understand and speak Black Lahu. When you see a tone mark in the phrases, try to use the correct pitch. Remember to attempt the right pitch for each syllable, instead of rising at the end of a question sentence or falling at the end of a statement sentence as in English. The two short tones are cut off by a catch at the end, rather like that in the middle of the expression of imminent danger, 'oh-oh!', or the Cockney replacement for 't' at the end of a word like 'fat'. The other five tones are longer, and in some cases have more pitch movement during the syllable: rising or falling as the case may be.

THE LANGUAGE
Lahu has substantial dialect differences, but the 'standard' dialect, understood by everyone, is Black Lahu. This is almost identical to Red Lahu and fairly similar to White Lahu and Shehleh. Yellow Lahu is quite distinct; fortunately most Yellow Lahu in Thailand have learned Black Lahu, so the visitor need only use the Black Lahu dialect.

Forming Sentences
Lahu, like Akha and Lisu, has the verb after the nouns in the sentence; so one says Nga‿ aw‿ca˅ ve, 'I rice eat', not 'I eat rice'. These languages have almost no complicated grammatical endings, though one can put an extra word in to show that a noun is the object: Nga‿ aw‿hta‿ ca˅ ve, on 'rice' in 'I eat rice' or that a verb is future Nga‿ aw‿ ca˅ tu‿ ve, 'I rice eat will'. These extra words follow the noun or verb that they accompany. Most sentences end with one or more final words; the most common is ve which expresses a positive fact or statement.

Adverbs and similar expressions come before the verb, most frequently at the beginning of the sentence: Ya₍nyi nga‿ aw‿ ca˅ ve, (today I rice eat). The negative comes immediately before the verb: Ya₍nyi nga‿ aw‿ ma˅ ca˅ (today I rice not eat); with the negative the usual final word ve is left off.

In Lahu, the pronouns nga‿, 'I'; naw‿, 'you'; yaw˅, 'he/she/ it', are often left out. The possessor comes first: naw‿ yeh‿, 'your house', and may be marked by ve: naw‿ ve yeh‿.

Classifiers

Like Thai and most other languages of this area, Lahu must have a classifier (counting word) after every number. In Lahu, Akha and Lisu, like Thai, this combination of number plus classifier follows the noun: chaw te˅ g̊a˅ (person one classifier), 'one person'. The choice of classifiers is wide, but for most nouns one can simply use a general classifier, Lahu ma‿ – chaw te˅ ma‿ is not the best Lahu, but it is understandable. The most common classifiers are g̊a˅ for people, hkeh for animals and shi_ for fruit; other than these ma‿ is quite acceptable.

Questions

When asking a question in Lahu, there are two different words at the end of the sentence: one for questions with a yes/no answer, la˅, and the other for questions containing a question word like 'who', 'what' and so on, le. Unlike many European languages,

Question Words	
who?	a‿ shu
what?	a‿ hto₍ma
when?	hk'a˅ hta^
where?	hk'aw_ /hk'a‿ lo
how much?	hk'a‿ ma
how many? [+ classifier]	hk'a‿ nyi˅
which ...?	hk'a‿ ve ...

there are no changes in the order of words in questions; so 'Will you eat rice?' is Naw‿ aw‿ ca˘ tu‿ la˘? (literally: you rice eat will question) while 'Who will eat rice?' is A shu aw‿ ca˘ tu‿ le? (literally: who rice eat will question). These question words may be used after ve or some other final words, or the ve may be omitted. If you want to ask how to say something, you can say: Chi te˘ma‿ a‿ hto∧ma le? 'What is this thing?'

When making a request or command, the final ve is left off; to be polite, one should instead add meh‿: Aw‿ ca˘ meh‿ (literally: rice eat please), 'Please eat rice'. Lahu is very rich in modal elements, most of which follow the verb; for example, hpeh∧, 'be able to'; ga˘, 'want to'; ja˘, 'very'; but a few come before it, such as g'a, 'have to'.

To Be

The verb 'to be' is like the modal 'be able to', hpeh∧; but as in Thai and most languages of the area, it is very infrequent because it is not used with adjectives which are verbs in their own right, nor with existentials which instead use the verb caw˘ ('have'):

Ca˘tu‿ da∧ ja˘!   The food (is) very good!
I˘ka^ caw‿ la˘?   Is there/Do you have water?

References

For further information, there is a *Lahu-Thai-English Dictionary* by Paul Lewis (Thailand Lahu Baptist Convention, PO Box 91, Chiang Mai 50000, 1986). A superb and much more compendious reference is *The Dictionary of Lahu* by James Matisoff (University of California Press, 1988). Matisoff has also written what may be the best grammar of any language; *The Grammar of Lahu* (University of California Press, revised 2nd edition, 1982).

WORDS & PHRASES
Greetings & Civilities

How are you? (lit: is life easy?)   Cheh˘ sha la˘?
Fine. (lit: life is easy)   Cheh˘ sha la˘.

Where are (you) going?   Hk'aw‿ k'ai le?

(I'm) going to ...   ... k'ai ve.
   the Lahu village   la˘ hu‿ hk'a^
   wash [oneself, not clothes]   i‾ka^ heh‾
   the Akha village   taw‿ kaw hk'a^
   home   a‾hk'aw

Where have (you) come from?   Hk'aw‿ ka∧ la‿ le?

I've come ...   ... la‿ ve.
   for a visit   ca gui˘
   from the North Thai village   kaw‾law‾ hk'a^ka∧

Have (you) eaten (rice)?   (Aw‿) ca˘ peu‿ o‿ la˘?
(I've) eaten (rice).   (Aw‿) ca˘ peu‿ o‿ .
(I) haven't eaten (rice).   (Aw‿) ma˘ ca˘ she‿?

Come inside the house!   A‾hk'aw la‿!
   [you should take off your shoes before entering]

LAHU

LAHU

Sit down inside the house!	A–hk'aw mui!
Drink (some) tea!	La‿g'ui‿daw‿.
Drink (some) water!	I⁻ ka^ daw‿!

Very good!	Da‿ja˘!
Thank you.	Aw‿ bon ui_ja˘!

(lit: blessing is very big – this phrase is mainly used by
Christians)

You're welcome.	Te‿chi⁻ ma˘ he^!

(lit: it's nothing)

Goodbye.	K'aw⁻eh‿ ve.

(lit: (I'm) going back)
[said by person who is leaving]

Goodbye!	A yeh⁻ k'ai meh‿.

(lit: please go slowly)
[said by person who is staying]

Small Talk

What is your name?	Naw‿ aw‿ meh a‿ hto‿ ma meh ve le?
My name is ...	... meh ve.
Where do you live?	Naw‿ cheh‿ kui‿ hk'a‿ lo cheh˘ ve le?
I live at ...	Nga‿ ... mvuh˘mi‿ lo cheh˘ve.

WHICH LANGUAGE?	
(I) don't understand.	Na ma˘ g'a.
Do you know ...?	Naw‿ ... shi‿ a‿ la˘?
English	Ka⁻la˘hpu hkaw˘
Thai	Htai˘ hkaw˘
Chinese	Heh^pa_hkaw˘
Burmese	Man hkaw˘

Have you got a ...? (lit: are they alive?)	Naw‿ ... caw‿ la˘?
wife	mi˘ma
husband	haw‾ hk'a^pa_
brothers and sisters	aw‿ vi‾ aw‿ nyi
mother and father	aw‿ pa aw‿ e
sons and daughters	ya˘pa‿ya˘mi˘

How many brothers and sisters do you have?	Aw‿vi‾ aw‿ nyi hk'a‿ nyi˘ g'a‾ caw‿le?
How many children do you have?	Ya‾pa‿ya˘mi˘ hk'a‿ nyi˘ g'a‾ caw‿le?

(I have) only one (person).	Te˘g'a‾ ti‾ caw‿.
(I have) four (people).	Awn_g'a‾ caw‿.

Accommodation & Meals

May I sleep in your house?	Naw‿ a‾hk'aw zuh_hpeh_ tu‿ la˘?
Where shall I put my things down?	Nga‿ maw‾ hk'a‿ lo teh ta_tu‿ le?
If I stay one night, how much is it?	Te‾ha‾ha‾k'o aw‿hpfuh˘ hk'a‿ ma yu‿le?
One night is 20 baht.	Te‾ha‾ nyi˘chi ba_.

Do you have (a) ...?	... caw‿la˘?
blanket	a‾bo_
flashlight (torch)	da^ mi_
lamp	kaw^f ai˘
mat	gu‾ye^
mattress	hpa‿teh
mosquito net	hpa‿ka_
pillow	u‾geh˘

How much is ...?	... hk'a‿ ma le?
one	te˘ ma‿
one animal	te˘ hkeh
one kg	te˘ ki˘lo‾

LAHU

SOME USEFUL WORDS

to sell	hawnˇve
to buy	vui˯ ve
to meet	maw˯ da˄ve
to give	piˇve
to take	yu˯ ve
to be happy	ha leh˯ ve
to be sad	dawˇha_ve
to remember	dawˇnawˇve
forget	leunˇve
to have a conversation	na˄u¯ te da˄ve
quickly	ha^ha^
slowly	a yeh¯yeh¯
country/nation	mvuhˇmi˯
town	meunˇ
market	tcuh
silver	hpu
gold	shi
this	chi ve
that	oˇve

Can (you) give me ...?	... piˇ laˇ tu˯ laˇ?
a banana	a¯pawˇk'u
a bowl	hkehˇ
chopsticks	a¯cu ka
a teacup	la˯ hkeh
fruit	i¯shi_
hot water	g'ui˯ haw
a (small) knife	a¯ hte˄ (eh¯)
a spoon	lu¯k'u
Will (you) make me ...?	... te laˇ tu˯ laˇ?
beans	naw^shi_
curry	aw_chiˇ

pork curry	va‸sha_aw_chiˇ
chicken curry	g'a^sha_aw_chiˇ
eggplant	ma⁻hkui⁻shi_
jackfruit	nu⁻feu⁻k'o_shi_
pumpkin	hpui⁻mui⁻shi_
(cooked) rice	aw_
taro	pehˇshi_
vegetables	g'awˇnaw g'awˇca⁻

Can I buy ...?	... vui‿hpeh‸tu‿laˇ?
batteries (flashlight)	da^ mi_shi_
a chicken	g'a‸te⁻hkeh
egg(s)	g'a^ u
fish	ngaˇ
(some) meat	aw‿sha_
pork	va‸sha_
soap	sa_bu_

Do you smoke tobacco?	Naw‿shu⁻daw‿laˇ?
I don't smoke tobacco.	Nga‿shu⁻ma⁻daw‿.
I don't want to smoke tobacco.	Nga‿shu⁻ma⁻daw‿gaˇ.
I don't smoke opium!	Nga‿ya fi_ ma⁻daw‿!

Are (you) sleepy?	Zuh‸ mui⁻geu‸laˇ?
(I) am very sleepy.	Zuh‸ mui⁻geu‸jaˇ.
(I) am very tired.	Heu‿jaˇve.

LAHU

AT THE TABLE

Please eat until you're full.	Aw_ caˇ bvuh^ meh_!
Drink whisky!	Tzuh‿daw‿!
I can't eat chillies.	A⁻hpe‸ca⁻ma⁻hpeh‸.
Have you got salt?	A⁻leh‸caw laˇ?
It's very delicious!	Meh_jaˇve.

Traditional Life & Crafts

Christian church	bon yeh ˍ
(lit: blessing house)	
Red Lahu temple	haw‾ yeh ˍ
(lit: palace house)	
Shehleh dancing ground	ca hkui^kui ˍ

Non-Christian celebrations usually take place on particular moon phase days; Christian church services are on Sundays. The major annual celebration is the New Year, just after the completion of harvest in late January to late February. This is celebrated by all Lahu groups with dancing around a decorated 'tree', playing traditional instruments, wearing traditional clothes and jewellery, and feasting. If possible you should time your visit to a Lahu village according to the phase of the moon or to see the New Year (or Christmas in a Christian village). Weddings are also festive occasions and worth seeing.

New Year	Hk'aw_∧suh_
celebrate	hk'aw_∧ ca˜ ve
(lit: eat the New Year)	
full moon [Shehleh holy day]	hapa taw ˍ
waning moon	hapa ya_∧ ve

LAHU

waning half-moon [Red Lahu holy day]	hapa che˰ ve
new moon [Shehleh holy day]	hapa suh_
waxing moon	hapa ta^ ve
eclipse of moon (lit: frog eats moon)	hapa pa_ caˇ ve

rice cakes	aw_hpfuh^

These are special for New Year, made of pounded sticky rice.

New Year tree	hk'aw˰cehˬ
God	G'uiˬsha
non-Christian spirit [ancestors, natural features]	neˇ
Red Lahu priest	to bo pa_
Sheleh priest	keh lon¯
non-Christian shaman/ traditional doctor	maw¯pa_
Christian pastor/teacher	sha_la_
Red, White Lahu ritual pillar [outside temple]	k'aw moˇtweh_

drum	cehnˬ
flute	leh¯
gong	jo lo
gourd reed-organ	naw_
jew's-harp	a¯htaˇ
loom	ca–mvuhˇ

Do (you) want to buy a ...?	... vuiˬgaˇ laˇ?

(I) want to buy a ...	... vuiˬgaˇ ve.
belt	ha_ pi ca^
bracelet	leh˰k'awˬ
button	ti¯hk'a^ shi_
leggings	hkui dawˇ
necklace [large, silver and decorative]	k'awˬpe ca^

pants	ha‿ htaw¯
purse	mi¯chaw eh¯
ring	la˄ pe‿
rupee [large silver coin]	hpu teh˄
shirt	a¯po˄
shoulder bag	mi¯chaw

LAHU

How much is it?	(Aw‿hpfuh˘) hk'a‿ma pi˘ tu‿ le?

white	hpu ve
black	na˄ ve
red	nyi ve
yellow	shi ve
blue/green	naw ve
beautiful	nyi sha ve
not beautiful	nyi ma˘ sha

Health

My ... hurts.	Nga‿ ... na‿ ve.
ear	na_paw
eye(s)	meh˄shi_
head	o¯k'o_
heart	nyi ma shi_
leg/foot	hkui sheh

lower back	caw^
stomach	g'o˘pe˯
tooth	ci˯
(My) arm is broken.	La^sheh hteh ve.
(I) have malaria.	Na˯hpeu^ ve.
(I) have diarrhoea.	G'o˘pe˯lon ve.
(I) am constipated.	G'o˘pe˯heh ve.
Have you got ...?	Naw˯ ... caw˯la˘?
medicine	na^ tsuh˘
a doctor	maw¯
Can (you) carry me?	Nga˯ hta^ pfuh˘ hpeh^ tu˯ la˘?
Wash (one's) hands.	La^sheh tsuh˘ve.
Wash (one's body).	I¯ka^ heh¯ve.
Go to excrete [euphemistic] (lit: go outside)	A¯k'a^ k'ai ve.
Go to urinate.	Tzuh˘ pi¯ve.

Directions & the Countryside

Where is the path to ...?	... k'ai ve ya^ k'aw hk'a˯ lo le˘?
the Karen village	yan˘hk'a^
the bus	lo^ meh
Is the path good?	Ya^ k'aw da^ la˘?
Not so good.	Tsuh˘tsuh¯ ma˘da^.
Go straight ahead.	Hte˘ eh˯ k'ai.
Can a motorcycle go there?	Maw_htaw_sai_k'ai hpeh^ tu˯ la˘?
Can you take me there by motorcycle?	Naw˯ maw_taw_ sai_geh_ feu hpeh^ tu˯la˘?
Will you come with me?	Naw˯ nga˯ geh k'ai tu˯ la˘?
Can you carry my things?	Naw˯ nga˯ maw˘ pfuh˘ hpeh^ tu˯ la˘?

LAHU

How much (money) should I give you?	Naw˰ hta˄ hk'a˰ ma g'a pi˜la˅ le?
side/direction	aw˰ hpaw˜
right side	la˄ sha hpaw˜
left side	la˄ meh_hpaw˜
above	aw˰ hta^hpaw˜
below	aw˰ haw˜ hpaw˜
in front	aw˰ g'u˜suh
behind	aw˰ hk'aw˄naw˜
to go	k'ai ve
[away from where speaker is now]	
to come	la˰ ve
[towards where speaker is now]	
to go up	ta^ve
to go down	ya˄ve
bridge	co˰
cliff	ha˜ hpaw˜
[unirrigated, sloping] field	heh
[irrigated, flat] field	ti mi_
fire	a˰mi_
moon	ha pa
mountain	hk'aw
path	ya˄k'aw
river/stream	i˜ka˜law˰
rock	ha˜pui shi_
smoke	mvuh˜hk'aw˜
sun	mvuh˜nyi
tree	suh^ceh˰
valley	law˰

LAHU

Weather

The sun is shining.	Mvuh˜ cha cha ve.
It's raining.	Mvuh˜_ye˰ la˰ ve.

It's hailing.	Va˘shi_k'a ve.
It's foggy.	Mo⌣ fi^ ve.
The path is slippery.	Ya∧k'aw le^ ve.
(I'm) cold.	Ka^ ve.
(I'm) hot.	Hawn ve.
(I'm/It's) wet.	Neh^ ve.

Ethnic Groups

[person: add chaw after the name; village: add hk'a^]

Lahu	La˘hu_
Akha	Taw⌣ kaw
Lisu	Li_shaw˘
Meo (Mong)	Hkeh meo^
Yao (Mien)	Hkeh yao^
Shan	Pi˘chaw˘
Northern Thai	Kaw_law¯
Thai	Htai˘
Chinese	Heh^pa_
Karen	Yan˘
Indian (lit: black Indian)	Ka˘la˘na^
European (lit: white Indian)	Ka˘la˘hpu

People

person	chaw
friend	aw⌣ chaw˘
man	haw¯ hk'a^pa_
woman	ya˘mi˘k'eh∧
old man	chaw maw˘
old woman	api
headman	hk'a^sheh pa_
baby	aw⌣ eh¯
young unmarried man chaw ha¯ pa_	
young unmarried woman ya˘mi˘ha¯	

LAHU

Animals

barking deer [small deer]	tsuh pi¯ k'weh∧
bear	yeh˛ mi ¯ taw_
bee	peh˘
bird	nga^ [Red Lahu ngeh^]
cat [dialect differences]	meh¯ nyi (black)
	mi˘ mi (red)
cattle	nu˘
dog	hpui˘
elephant	hawn
a fly	pui¯
gibbon	maw∧na^
horse	i¯ mvuh˘
jungle fowl	heh¯ g'a^
leech	ve∧
louse	she˛
monkey	maw∧
mule	law_
porcupine	fa^pu
rat	fa^cha∧

roach	pi¯ pa
sambar deer [large deer]	hkui¯ zuh ˬ
snake	vui ˬ
squirrel	fa^htaw^
tiger	la˘
water buffalo	awn¯ k'a_
wild boar	heh¯ va^

Numbers & Classifiers

Counting in Lahu requires a classifier after the number. Both number and classifier follow the noun, so La˘hu_te˘g̓a˘, 'one Lahu' is literally 'Lahu-one-human'. The common classifier is maˬ, except with three, four and sometimes nine which may use leh˘ instead. With numbers ending in a zero, the classifier is not needed. Animals are better counted with the classifier hkeh, people with g'a˘, fruit or small round things with shi_, and Thai money (Baht) with ba^ instead of maˬ.

1	te˘maˬ	6	hkaw^ maˬ
2	nyi˘maˬ	7	suh_maˬ
3	shehleh˘	8	he¯ maˬ
4	awn_leh˘	9	k'aw˘maˬ
5	nga˘maˬ	10	te˘chi (lit: 1, 10)

The rounded numbers are made with the number plus the number 10, chi:

30	sheh chi (lit: 3, 10)	90	k'aw˘chi (lit: 9, 10)

The hundreds are similarly combined from the number plus 100, ha; thousands are the number plus 1000, hin¯; and tens of thousands are the number plus 10,000, meun_:

100	te˘ha	500	nga˘ha
2000	nyi˘hin¯	10,000	te˘meun_

LAHU

Combinations go from largest to smallest:

1998	teˇhin⁻ k'awˇha k'awˇchi he⁻ hk'aw_∧
555	ngaˇha⁻ ngaˇchi ngaˇma ◡
35	shehchi ngaˇma ◡

Time Words

Basic time words can also be used as classifiers:

day	nyi
10 days	teˇchi nyi
night	ha⁻
month	hapa
four months	awn_ hapa
year	hk'aw_∧
six years	hkaw_∧ hk'aw_∧
yesterday	a⁻ nyi
today	ya_∧ nyi
tomorrow	shaw⁻ paw_
day after tomorrow	hpa^nyi
this morning	ya_∧ shaw⁻
this evening	ya_∧ pui⁻

LAHU

CULTURE, SUBGROUPS & LOCATIONS

This group calls itself Akha (with both syllables spoken on a low tone). The Thai groups in South-East Asia call them Kaw or Ekaw (Igor), a name the Akha do not like. Those who live in the southern part of Yunnan (in the Xishuangbanna area) are designated as Aini or Yani by the Chinese, but they call themselves Akha, the same as those in Myanmar (Burma), Thailand and Laos do.

The Akha numbered about 600,000 in 1998. Over 300,000 of these live in south central and southern Yunnan in China, and some 200,000 live in Kengtung state, Myanmar. There are 55,000 in Thailand and 65,000 in Laos. There's a very closely related group, living in China in the Red River area, called Hani (pronounced *K'a ˅ nyi ˅* if we use Akha writing); Za˅ nyi˅ is the old Akha name for themselves, still used in poetic language. These Hani number an additional 1.2 million people, of whom about 900,000 speak dialects close to Akha.

Most Akha in Thailand live in Chiang Rai province. The main concentration of Akha villages is to the west of the road from Chiang Rai to Mae Sai, and north of the Mae Kok River. There are more and more Akha villages now located south of the Mae Kok in Chiang Rai province, as well as in the northern part of Chiang Mai province, and a scattering of Akha villages in the provinces of Lampang and Tak.

There are many Akha villages on or near the road that goes from Mae Chan up to Mae Salong. Just four km before reaching the town of Mae Sai (due north of Chiang Rai town), there's a road off to the left (going west), which leads to the village of Pa Mi Akha. The headdresses of the women in this village are quite different from those worn by U˅ Lo˅ and Loi Mi women.

An Akha village can be identified by its gates, the towering village swing, and the distinctive style of the houses with their massive roofs. The first house to be built in a village must be that of the **dzoe˅ma** ('village founder'). The rest of the houses tend to

Akha (Ikaw) in Thailand

MYANMAR

Chiang Rai

LAOS

Mae Hong Song

Phayao

Chiang Mai

Nan

Lamphun

Lampang

Phrae

Uttaradit

Loei

Tak

Sukhotai

Phitsanulok

Phetchabun

Kamphaeng Phet

Phichit

Nakhon Sawan

THAILAND

Uthai Thani

ANDAMAN SEA

Suphan Buri

Kanchanaburi

BANGKOK

Ratchaburi

Phetchaburi

Bight of Bangkok

AKHA

0   100   200 km

be grouped around his. An Akha village will often have more than one name. The name in Thai may reflect some physical feature, such as Cogon Grass Village or Elephant Mountain Village. When the Akha use the Thai name, they will put Akha at the end of it. For example, 'cogon grass' in Thai would be pronounced ba_v ka^v by the Akha, so for the Cogon Grass Village they'll say Ba_v ka^v A_vka_v.

Often they refer to a village by the name of its founder or current headman. When this is done they use the word **pu** ('village') at the end. For example, in the village where A_v baw^v Meh^v is headman, it's called A_vbaw^v Meh^v**pu**.

Traditional Akha houses are made with wooden house posts, thatched roofs, and most everything else bamboo. Akha houses have no windows, and the roof is constructed in such a way that the eaves come down very low on both sides and ends. This results in a dark interior, but keeps out the wind and rain, and provides a work space outside under the eaves. Houses are usually built up on posts, although sometimes the side on the upper slope of the mountain is built directly on the ground, while the downhill side is elevated. Space under the houses affords a convenient shelter for the animals, as well as storage space for firewood and equipment.

There are two main sections in an Akha house, the men's and the women's, with a shoulder-high partition between the sections extending as far as the central house beam. In non-Christian homes, an a_v poe_v paw_^ law_^ ('ancestral altar') is hung on the women's side of the partition. This ancestral altar (which is usually just a section of bamboo covered by a leaf, but is sometimes a small shelf) gives an aura of sacredness to the house. It's the most sacred part of their home and it must never be touched by an outsider.

It is improper for an outsider to walk through an Akha house, entering one door and leaving by the other. It's also not acceptable for a person to go directly through an Akha village without entering some home and having at least a drink of water. Food

AKHA

or drink will always be offered in an Akha home, and it is important for the guest to partake, even if only a token amount. Otherwise it appears to the Akha that the visitor is an intruder – perhaps even a thief. Male guests should not enter the women's section of the house unless invited to do so by the head of the household. Women visitors, on the other hand, can enter the men's section along with other visitors.

A well-dressed Akha woman's clothes are stunning, from her elaborate headdress to her ornate leggings. Her basic costume consists of a headdress, a jacket worn over a halter-like garment (more often a T-shirt these days), a short skirt, a sash with decorated ends, and leggings. The Akha man's clothing isn't so elaborate, but there's a certain smartness in the cut of his jacket and the tilt of his turban – at least when he dons his Akha clothing. The basic material used in Akha clothing is a firmly woven homespun cotton cloth, dyed with indigo to a blue-black hue.

In Thailand there are three major styles of dress for the Akha:

U∨Lo∨
    this style, which literally means 'pointed headdress', has developed among most of the Akha who have been living in Thailand for many years. Representatives from some 25 or so clans dress in this style.

Loi Mi (Law Mi∨ Sha^)
    this style is named after a large mountain in Kengtung State, Myanmar, from which many of these people come, called Loi Mi Mountain. It includes most of those who have migrated recently from Myanmar. This group is sometimes called U∨ Bya∨, 'flat headdress' Akha by those living in Thailand.

Pa∨Mi∨
    this style is named after one village in Thailand, although it's not limited to that village. This style is worn primarily by women of the Mah∨ Po^ clan, whether in China, Myanmar or Thailand, and is the one dress style which tends to be used by a single clan or two. The dialect spoken by these Akha is virtually the same as what the Chinese call 'Aini Akha'.

Each Akha is a member of a patrilineal clan. There are well over 100 different clans among the Akha, although all are not present in Thailand. In Thailand the clan name is often used for the family name in official papers. (For more on clan and lineages, see the *Akha-English-Thai Dictionary* by Lewis.)

The Akha week (following the Chinese) contains 12 days named after animals. These are the same names, and in the same order, as the names of years in the 12-year cycle. The fifth day and fifth year are named 'forgotten' after a mythical, unknown animal.

1	nyo˅	buffalo		7	yaw˅	sheep
2	k'a˅ la˅	tiger		8	myo˄	monkey
3	tah˅ la˄	mule		9	za	chicken
4	lah˅	rabbit		10	kui˅	dog
5	sheh˅	forgotten		11	za˄	pig
6	mah˅	horse		12	ho	rodent

Most Akha have nine major ancestral offerings, a_v poe_v law^v-eu, each year, which are very important to the Akha who follow the 'Akha Way' – the traditional Akha lifestyle. These are primarily for family members (outsiders are not allowed in the house when the offering is being made). Villagers don't go to the fields to work on these days. There's not much for outsiders to see or participate in during these offerings, with the exception of Ka^v yeh^yeh^-eu. The dates of these offerings vary from village to village, as they must be on an 'auspicious day' of the dzoe_v ma, 'village founder':

AKHA

Ga⌄ tah⌄ pa⌄ -eu
  the offering for the New Year. This is not spectacular like
  Lisu and Lahu New Years. The date differs from village to
  village, but is usually in December or January.

K'm⌄ shui∧
  an offering to help hunters (they colour chicken eggs at this time)

K'm⌄ mi⌄
  in honour of the village founder

Ceh⌄ ka
  rice planting

Yeh⌄ ku⌄
  women's New Year, when they swing on the village swing.
  This helps the villagers' health.

Zaw la la-eu
  an offering made to help ensure plentiful crops

Ya ci ∧ci ∧-eu
  the chicken-plucking offering

Ka⌄ yeh∧yeh∧-eu
  driving the evil spirits out of their village. This is interesting
  to watch.

Ceh⌄ nm⌄
  offering for the new rice

There are also the following major village ceremonies:

Law⌄kah⌄ m⌄-eu
  this is the renewal of the village gate (law⌄ kah⌄)

Mi⌄ sah⌄ cu⌄ sah⌄ law⌄ -eu
  this is an offering to the 'lords and rulers of land and water'
  performed at a special tree out in the jungle. (Note this is
  often just called 'Mi⌄ sah⌄ law⌄ -eu'.

It is generally permitted for outsiders to be present in these two
ceremonies, but nothing must be touched. Before taking pictures it would be polite to get permission, either from the **dzoe⌄
ma** ('village founder') or the **bu⌄seh⌄** ('village political headman').

AKHA

The Akha will realise that you cannot speak their language flaw-lessly, but there are certain taboo terms to steer clear of. For example, the words for: twins, hail, flowers, and certain other expressions having to do with taboo items in the Akha culture. Also, do *not* ask a man or woman the name of their spouse. This is very rude in Akha, and she or he will not be able to tell you – at least this is true among the non-Christian Akha. Almost any-thing having to do with death is best left unsaid – unless you hear the Akha say it. It is also very important to refer to the Akha as A$_\lor$ ka$_\lor$ (both low tones, the second syllable aspirated), and not as **Kaw** or **Ekaw**.

Remember too that those following the 'Akha Way' (A$_\lor$ ka$_\lor$ zah$^\lor$ taw$_\lor$ -eu) will be outraged if you do anything to hurt their sacred objects and places:

- The ancestral altar in each home (a$_\lor$ poe$_\lor$ paw$_\land$ law$_\land$) – must not be touched.

- The village gate(s) (law$^\lor$ kah$_\lor$) – these and everything related to them (such as the figures) must not be touched. Note: There's also a ka$^\lor$ yeh$^\land$ law$^\lor$ kah$_\lor$, which has wooden 'spears' they have made for the ka$^\lor$yeh$^\land$ ceremony.

- The village swing (la$_\land$ ceu$_\lor$) – this must not be swung on any time of the year except when the swing ceremony is being held.

- The village water source (i$^\lor$ cu$_\land$ law$^\lor$ k'aw$_\land$) – no relieving oneself in its vicinity. The special tree near the village where an annual ceremony is held for the 'lords of land and water' (mi $^\lor$ sah$^\lor$ law$^\lor$ du$_\land$) – this tree will be fenced off and the area should not be entered.

- The burial ground (lm$_\lor$ bym$^\lor$) – this area must not be burned or there will have to be a ceremony to rectify it.

Not only will they be outraged – they could also fine you. The fine would probably pay for the things they would need to repurify the object or area.

AKHA

Your sensitivity to their language and culture will be greatly appreciated by them, and make your stay more enjoyable. Please do not take a picture of any pregnant women, or of anyone who does not want their picture taken. Often they have good reasons for this which they won't be able to convey to you, but which are important to them.

When entering an Akha village you will see children playing. Do nothing to startle or frighten them. If you should do that and they get sick later, the parents might think you frightened their child's soul away. When entering an Akha village it's good to say: **Ta_v gu^, ta_v gu^. Ta_v gu^ de.** 'Don't be afraid, don't be afraid. Please don't be afraid'.

AKHA

SOUNDS

The sounds of the Akha language can be represented by the writing system used in this phrasebook. There are many Christian Akha who can read it, along with a few non-Christian Akha as well. There's also a writing system for Akha using the Thai script.

Vowels

Akha has two types of vowels: oral and laryngealised (the latter is sometimes called glottalised, constricted, or 'creaky').

The oral vowels (very much like vowels in English) occur on three tones which tend to be quite level:

high	aˇ baˇ	shadow
mid	yaw ba	white/cream coloured
low	yaw ba˅	thin

The laryngealised vowels (which sound 'creaky' when spoken in isolation) occur on two tones:

mid	ba^ k'o^	skin, bark
low	ba˄ -eu	to carry (on one's shoulder)

The type of vowel used makes a difference to the consonant in the following cases:

- When there is an oral vowel following these consonants, they are aspirated.

- When there is a creaky vowel following these consonants, then no puff of air follows (unaspirated).

For more information on the pronunciation of aspirated and unaspirated sounds, see Consonants in this section, and the Introduction, page 15.

AKHA

There are 13 vowels in Akha, most of them like English:

i	as in beat
e	as in bait
eh	as in bet
u	as in boot
o	as in boat
a	as in ah
aw	as in bought
eu	something like 'book' in English, but said with the lips spread
ui	with the lips spread and tongue higher than in eu
ah	nazalised 'a' sound, as in French
oi	the tongue is in the position of saying 'i', but the lips are in the position of saying 'u', as in German 'ü' or French 'u'
oe	the tongue is in the position of saying 'e', but the lips are in the position of saying 'o', as in German 'ö' or French 'eu'

There is also a 'syllabic m' which functions as a vowel.

m$^\vee$-eu	to do
m$_\vee$	sky
lm$_\vee$bym$^\vee$	grave

There are three borrowed diphthongs: **ao** (as in 'ouch'), **ai** (as in 'eye'), **am** (an 'a' followed directly by a syllabic 'm').

Consonants

The consonants in Akha which are aspirated when they occur with oral (normal) vowels, but unaspirated with creaky vowels are:

	Aspirated	Unaspirated
p	pa$_\vee$	pa$_\wedge$
py	pya$_\vee$	pya$_\wedge$
t	ta$_\vee$	ta$_\wedge$
k	ka$_\vee$	ka$^\wedge$
ts	tsa$_\vee$	tsa$_\wedge$
c	ca$_\vee$	ca$_\wedge$
k	ka$_\vee$	ka$_\wedge$

AKHA

There is one other consonant **j** which is pronounced like the 'j' in English 'jaw' when it is an oral vowel, but which sounds more like 'dy-' when the vowel is creaky: **ja^-eu**.

The sound represented by **k'** is said far back in the throat, and is given a fricative quality (like the Scottish word 'loch', only at the beginning of the word instead of the end). Likewise, the sound of **g'** is similar to French 'r', with friction at the back.

The sound represented by **dz** combines two letters, but is only one sound. Think of 'your da*d's* office', then run the d's together. By eliminating the other sounds you will get something like the Akha word **dzaw**. The sound represented by **ts** also combines two letters, but is only one sound. Think of 'the goa*ts* odour', then run the t's together. By eliminating the other sounds you will get something like the Akha word **tso**.

C represents a sound like English 'ch', aspirated or unaspirated, and is not a 'k' sound as it sometimes is in English.

The following consonants are similar to certain English sounds: **my** (as in '*mu*sic'), **ny** (as in 'ca*ny*on'), **py** (as in '*pew*'), **b, d, g** (the hard 'g' as in 'get'), **z, y, l, s, sh, m, n** and **ng** (this comes at the beginning of syllables, unlike English). **By** is a sequence of 'b' plus 'y'.

THE LANGUAGE

The main dialect of Akha as spoken in Thailand, Myanmar, Laos and southern Yunnan province of China is the Jeu˅ G'oe˅ dialect. There are local variations which are usually not major, although one will recognise differences between the three major Akha groups in Thailand. The U˅ lo˅ group living in Thailand tends to merge some consonants together (especially among the younger generation).

Verbs

Akha, like Lahu and Lisu, has the verb after the nouns, adjectives and adverbs in the sentence. So one says: **Nga˅ haw˅ dza˅ ma**, 'I eat rice'. If one says **I˅ nah nga˅ haw˅ dza˅ ma**, 'Today I eat rice' the word for 'today', **i˅ nah**, must come at the beginning.

The word for 'eat', **dza˅**, is followed by a particle which shows that it is present tense, and that it is the speaker who is eating. If you speak of eating in the past, the ending would be ma_v: Nga^v haw$_v$ dza$_v$ ma$_v$ (note the low tone on the ma$_v$ at the end). If speaking of someone else eating, the ending will be **meh**: A$_v$ yaw$_\wedge$ haw$_v$dza$_v$meh, 'He/She eats rice'. If the other person is finished eating, A$_v$ yaw$_\wedge$ haw$_v$ dza$_v$ meh$_v$. For the negative, ma$_v$ comes immediately before the verb: I$_v$ nah nga^v haw$_v$ ma$_v$ dza$_v$ -a, 'Today I do not eat rice'.

The common particle that is used with a verb is -eu, as in la^v-eu, 'to come'; daw^v-eu , 'to drink' and dza$_v$ -eu, 'to eat'; although the -eu is not always used in sentences.

Pronouns

Any recipient of an action is indicated by the -ah^v particle following the noun: Nga^v a$_v$ yaw$_\wedge$ -ah^v di$_v$ ma$_v$, 'I hit him'. The reason there's a hyphen is to show that the vowel ah^v doesn't begin with a 'glottal stop', but follows on with no break from the vowel preceeding it.

Another form of -eu is used to show possession : ie -eu$_v$: nga$_v$-eu$_v$, 'my'; naw$_v$ -eu$_v$, 'your', although again this may not be used every time. For example, nga$_v$-eu$_v$nym^v^{v}, 'my house'; nga$_v$ nym^v, 'my house' – but note the tone on nga$_v$ is still low.

Pronouns	
I	nga^v
you	naw^v
he/she/it	a$_v$ yaw$_\wedge$
we	nga ma$_\wedge$
you (plural)	naw ma$_\wedge$
they (he/she and I)	a$_v$yaw$_\wedge$ ma$_\wedge$
we (you and I)	a$_v$dui, a^{v}dui
two of us	nga nya$_\wedge$
the two of you	naw nya$_\wedge$
the two of them	a$_v$yaw$_\wedge$ nya$_\wedge$

Questions

When asking a question in Akha, there are three types of sentence patterns used for questions that demand an explanation:

1) The question that asks what or why:

What do you want?	A$_v$ je$_v$ geu$_\wedge$ maw$_\wedge$ nya.
Why don't you want to go?	A$_v$ je$_v$ mi ˇneh ma$_v$ i ˇmaw$_\wedge$ nya.

2) The question that asks for the number (a$_v$ mya$^\wedge$), the person (a$_v$ su$_v$), or which particular item (a$_v$ geu):

How many animals are there?	A^v mya $^\wedge$ maw^v jaw^v te.
Which person died?	A$_v$ su^v g'a$_v$ shi ˇta$_v$.
Where did you go?	A$_v$ geu ga^v le te$_v$.

In the first two examples a classifier 'counting word' must be used. The first is **maw**$_v$ to indicate animals, the second is **g'a**$_v$ to indicate humans:

3) The question that has to do with space and time:

How big is it?	A^v hui ah^v ta?
When did you come?	A^v myah la^v te$_v$?

There is another sentence pattern which demands a yes or no answer. The question ending for such sentences is **lo**^{v}:

Are you well?	Jaw^v sa^v do$^\wedge$ mi ˇ -a lo^v?
Right here?	Heu ga^v lo^v?
May I drink water?	Nga$_v$ i^v cu$_\wedge$ daw$_v$ nya meh lo^v?

Question Words

who?	a˅ su˅ g'a.
what?	a˅ je˅
when?	a˅ myah
where?	a˅ ga˅
how much?	a˅mya^
how many? [+ classifier]	a˅ mya^
which? [+ classifier]	a˅ geu

Politeness

The final particle **de** indicates politeness, and should be used quite often when speaking Akha, especially with those your own age and older. **K'oe˅ paw ta˅ i˅ de**, 'Please don't go there'.

If you are leaving an Akha village and going downhill, or to the south, you will say **G'o˄ -i˅ ma de**, 'I am returning down now' (polite).

If you are inviting someone to eat, you would say **Dza˅ -aw˅ de**. In this case, the -**aw˅** is a command word, which can sound rough and abrupt at times when used alone, but will be softened and polished by the **de** which follows it.

References

For further information, there's an *Akha-Thai-English Dictionary* by Paul Lewis, (Development & Agriculture Project for Akha, 115 M 2, T Rimkok, A Muang, Chiang Rai 57000, 1989). No comprehensive grammar is available, but many anthropologists have studied the Akha and some ethnographic films and books exist.

WORDS & PHRASES
Greetings & Civilities

Where are you going?	Naw˅a˅ ga˅ i ˅te?
(I) have come here.	Heu ga˅ la˅ma.

AKHA

(I) have come to your place.	Naw˅ jaw ˅ga˅ la˅-eu˅ ma.
(I'm) not going anywhere.	Ti˅ ga˅ -i˅ma˅ i˅.
(I'm) going to the mountain field.	Ya˅ngeh i˅ma.
(I'm) going to get firewood.	Mi˅ dza˅ k'eh^-i ˅ma.
(I'm) going to get water.	I˅ cu˄ k'aw˄-i ˅ ma.
(I'm) going to town.	Meu˅-ah ˅i ˅ma.

WHICH LANGUAGE?

Do you know the Akha language?	Naw˅ A˅ ka˅ daw˅si˅nya ma lo˅?
I know the Akha language.	Nga˅ A˅ ka˅ daw˅ si˅ nya ma.
I do not yet know the Akha language.	Nga˅ A˅ ka˅ daw˅ ma˅ si˅ nya si˅.
I know a little Akha.	Nga˅ A˅ ka˅ daw˅ui cui^ si˅ nya ma.
I know only a little Akha.	Nga˅ A˅ ka˅daw˅ ui cui ^ teh˅-eh˅ si˅ nya ma.
Do you know the Thai language?	Tai˅ daw˅ si˅ nya ma lo˅?
I know the Thai language.	Nga˅ Tai˅daw˅ si˅nya ma.
I don't know the Thai language.	Nga˅ Tai˅ daw˅ma˅ si˅ nya.
I do not know written Thai.	Nga Tai˅ sah˅ bo˄ ma˅ si˅ nya.
Do (you) understand?	G'o^ shaw nya ma lo˅?
I do not understand.	Nga˅ ma˅ g'o^ shaw nya nya.

AKHA

AKHA

To make it more polite, **de** can be added to all of the positive sentences. See page 55 for an explanation.

(I) bow my head in greeting   U˅ du˅ tah˅ ma.
(to you).

(I) bow my head in greeting   U˅ du˅tah˅ ma de.
(to you too).

Thank (you).   Gui˅lah˅hui˅miˇ-a de.
(lit: great blessing/value – this is often said to a person who
is staying behind)

Thank (you) very much indeed!   Gui˅lah˅hui˅dui dui ma.
Never mind.   Ti˅je˅-i˅ma˅ngeuˇ.
[used both in answer to the 'thanks', and as we would use
'never mind' in English]

Are you well?	Jaw˅ sa˅do^ mi˅-a lo˅?
(lit: living easily?)	
I am well.	Jaw˅sa˅do^mi˅-a.
I am not well.	Jaw˅sa˅ma˅ do^nya.
(I) have come (up) for a visit.	Daw˅deh g'a la˅-eu˳ma.
Please come (to) sit in	I˅kah˅nui˅la˅-aw˅de.
the house.	
Please drink some tea.	Law˅baw˅ daw˅-aw˅de.
Please drink some water.	I˅cu˄daw˅-aw˅de.
Please eat some fruit.	A˅si˅dza˅-aw˅de.
Thanks.	Gui˅lah˅ hui˅teh˄-a.
[with the idea that there will be blessing/value involved]	

Do (you) know?	Si˅ nya ma lo˅?
(I) know.	Si˅ nya ma.
(I) do not know.	Ma˅ si˅ nya nya.
He/She knows.	A˅ yaw˄ si˅ nya meh.
He/She does not know.	A˅ yaw˄ ma˅ si˅ nya-a.

(I) am returning (down) now.	G'o˄-i˅ma de.
(I) am returning (up) now.	G'o˄ le˅ ma de.
[said by those leaving]	

Go slowly back down.	Aw law^law^-eh˅ g'o˄ -i˅ de.
Go slowly back up.	Aw law^law^-eh˅ g'o˄ le˅ de.
[said by those remaining behind]	

Small Talk

What is your name?	Naw˅ -eu˅ tsaw˅ myah a˅ jo^-eh˅ ku˅ te?
My name is ...	Nga˅ -eu˅ tsaw˅ myah˅ -a˅, ... leh˅ ku˅ -eu meh.
My name is Li Nah˅.	Li Nah˅ leh˅ ku ˅-eu meh.
[a boy's name]	
My name is Mi˅Nah˅.	Mi˅ Nah˅ leh˅ ku˅ -eu meh.
[a girl's name]	

AKHA

What village do (you) live in?	A$_\vee$ geu pu -ah$^\vee$ jaw$^\vee$ te?
What are (you) looking for?	A$_\vee$ je$_\vee$ po^-eu cah te?
Is (your) field good?	Ya$^\vee$ yaw mui$_\vee$ nga lo$^\vee$?
(It) is good.	Yaw mui$_\vee$ nga.
Not all that good.	Teu na^ na^ -eh$^\vee$ ma$_\vee$ mui$_\vee$ -a.
Not all that good.	Ti$_\vee$ paw^-i$_\vee$ ma$_\vee$ mui$_\vee$ -a.
(There are) many rocks.	K'a$_\vee$ lo yaw mya$_\vee$ meh.
Is that so (OK)?	Ngeu$^\vee$ ma lo$^\vee$?

[when speaking of oneself, otherwise it will be:
Ngeu$^\vee$meh lo.]

It is so.	Ngeu$^\vee$ ma.
It is not so.	Ma$_\vee$ ngeu$^\vee$.
Have (you) planted rice (yet)?	Ceh$^\vee$ ka ta$_\vee$ ma$_\vee$ lo$^\vee$?
(I) haven't planted rice yet.	Ceh$^\vee$ ma$_\vee$ ya ka-a$_\vee$ si$_\vee$.
(I) have planted rice.	Ceh$^\vee$ ka ji$^\vee$ ma$_\vee$.

AKHA

Note: For most animate objects jaw˅ is used, for inanimate objects ja^ is used.

How many children do you have?	Naw˅ za˅ a˅ mya^ g'a˅ jaw˅ te?
I have two boys and two girls.	Nga˅ a˅li nyi˅ g'a˅, a˅ bu˅ nyi˅ g'a˅ jaw˅ ma.
I have no children yet.	Nga˅ za˅ ti˅ g'a˅ -i˅ ma˅ jaw˅ le si˅.

Is your father present (alive)?	Naw˅ da jaw˅ meh lo?
My father is present (alive).	Nga˅ da jaw˅ meh.
Do (you) have a father?	A˅ da baw ma lo˅?
(I) have a father.	A˅ da baw ma.
Do (you) have a mother?	A˅ ma baw ma lo˅?
I do not have a mother since she has died.	A˅ ma shi˅-eu˅ mi˅ neh ma˅ baw-a.

How old are (you)?	A˅ k'o˄ a˅ mya^ k'o˄ k'aw^ la˅ -eu˅ te?
(I) am over 20 years old.	A˅ k'o˄ nyi˅ tse˅ dzeh˅ -i˅ma˅.

Accommodation & Meals

Do (you) want to stay overnight?	Ya˄ maw˄ mi˅-a lo˅?
(I) want to stay overnight.	Ya˄ maw˄ mi˅-a.
(I) cannot stay overnight.	Ma˅ ya˄ nya-a.
Thank you very much. [polite]	Gui˅ lah˅ hui˅ ma de.
I want to stay one or two nights.	Ti˅ mi˅ nyi˅ mi˅ ya˄ maw˄ mi˅-a de.

How much (money) do (you) want?	A˅ poe˅ a˅ mya^ geu˄ ma˅ nya?
Fifty baht should be enough.	Nga˅ tse˅ ba˄ lo˄ du˅.
(I) want to ask (beg) 60 baht.	Ko˄ tse˅ ba˄ sha˄ maw˄ mi˅- a.

Do (you) want rice liquor?	Ji˅ ba˅ daw˅ maw˄ mi˅-a lo˅?
I do not want to drink rice liquor.	Nga˅ ji˅ ba˅ ma˅ daw˅ maw˄ nya.
Do you want to smoke ('drink') opium?	Naw˅ ya pi˅ daw˅ maw˄ mi˅-a lo˅?
(I) don't want to smoke (it).	Ma˅ daw˅ maw˄ nya.
Do (you) want to drink tea?	Law˅ baw˅ daw˅ maw˄ mi˅-a lo˅?
(I) want to drink tea please.	Law˅ baw˅ daw˅ maw˄ mi˅ - a de.

AKHA

AT THE TABLE

Have (you) eaten rice yet?	Haw˅ dza˅ g'a˅ ma˅ lo˅?
(I) have eaten.	Dza˅ g'a˅ ma˅.
(I) have eaten morning rice.	Shaw˅ haw˅ dza˅ g'a˅ ma˅.
(I) have eaten noon rice.	G'ah˅ haw˅ dza˅ g'a˅ ma˅.
(I) have not eaten evening rice yet.	Ci˄ haw˅ ma˅ dza˅ -a˅ si˅.
Are you hungry?	Naw˅ haw˅ meh˄ nya lo˅?
I am hungry.	Nga˄ -ah˅ haw˅ meh˄ nya.
(I) am not hungry yet.	Ma˅ meh˄ nya si˅.
I am not hungry yet.	Nga˅ -ah˅ haw˅ ma˅ meh˄ nya si˅.
Are you thirsty?	I˅ cu˄ meh˄ mi˅ -a lo˅?
I am thirsty.	Nga˅ -ah˅ i˅ cu˄ meh˄ nya.
(I) am not thirsty yet.	Ma˅ meh˄ nya si˅.
(I) want to drink water.	I˅ cu˄ daw˅ maw˄ mi˅ -a.

What do you want to eat?	Naw˅ a˅ je˅ dza˅ maw˄ nya?
Do (you) have ...?	... ja˄ ma lo˅?
banana	nga beh˄
beans	a˅ nui˄
blanket	a˅ bui
bowl	k'm˅ ma˅
chicken eggs	ya u˄
chicken [meat]	ya ci˄ sha˅ ji˅
chilli	la˄ pi˅
chopsticks	ju da˅
fruit	a˅ si˅
knife	mi ceh˅
mat	gaw˅ pu
mushroom	a˅ hm˅

pillow	uᵥ g'mᵛ
(cooked) rice	hawᵥ
pork	aᵥ zaₐ shaᵥ jiᵛ
pumpkin	maᵛdeh
spoon	kuᵥ tsaₐ
stool	nuiᵛgawᵥ
taro	mahᵥ
vegetables	g'awᵛpaₐ
water	iᵛcuₐ

(I) do not (have it).	Maᵥ jaᴧ.
(I) do not have any more.	Maᵥ paᵛ jaᴧ.
(lit: I had them and they are gone)	
(I) have. [polite]	Jaᴧ ma de.
(I) would like to eat chicken.	Ya ciᴧ shaᵥ jiᵛ dzaᵥ mawₐ miᵛ-a de.

Shopping

AKHA

Is this shoulder bag expensive?	Pehᵛ tahᵛ heu aᵛ poeᵥ yaw k'aᴧ meh loᵛ?
It is not at all expensive.	Aᵛ poeᵥ tiᵥ pawₐ-iᵥ maᵥ k'aᴧ -a.
(I) will sell it for 70 baht.	Shiₐ tseᵛ baₐ ahᵥ nehᵥ ma.
Is it new?	Yaw shuiₐ meh loᵛ?
(It) is not new, (it) is old.	Yaw shuiₐ maᵥ ngeuᵛ. Yaw oeᵛ meh.
That is good. [this means you accept]	Yaw muiᵥ nga.
I will give 70 baht. [polite ending]	Ngaᵛ shiₐ tseᵛ baₐ biₐ ma de.

AKHA

SOME USEFUL WORDS

to sell	ah$_\vee$-eu
to buy	zeu$^\vee$-eu
to give	bi$_\wedge$-eu
to take	yu$^\vee$-eu
to meet up with	tah$_\vee$ pu$_\vee$-eu
to go to market	leh^ dzu$_\wedge$-eu
town	meu$_\vee$
to converse	daw$_\vee$ ja ja-eu
to remember	noe$_\vee$ ta$_\vee$-eu
to forget	ngeh$^\vee$-eu
to relieve oneself	ga$^\vee$nyi$^\vee$i$^\vee$-eu
country/nation	mi$^\vee$k'ah$_\vee$
this	heu
that	k'oe$^\vee$
here	heu ga$^\vee$
there	k'oe$^\vee$ ga$^\vee$
quickly	yaw kaw kaw-eh$^\vee$
slowly	aw law^ law^-eh$^\vee$
tired	g'a$_\vee$ doe$^\vee$doe$^\vee$-eu
worried, sad	noe$_\vee$ sha$_\vee$-eu
silver/white/money	pyu$^\vee$
gold/yellow	shui$^\vee$
tasty	yaw kui$^\vee$ or kui$^\vee$-eu
straight	yaw daw$^\vee$ or daw$^\vee$ coe ni
happy	la$_\vee$k'a$_\vee$ceh$^\vee$-eu

belt	jo$_\wedge$ pa$_\wedge$
bracelet	la$_\wedge$ du$_\wedge$
drum	tah$_\vee$
flute	meh$_\vee$li$^\vee$
gong	boe loe
gourd reed-organ	la$_\wedge$ je$_\vee$

jew's-harp	ja˅oe˅
leggings [man's]	kui˅taw^
leggings [woman's]	kui˅bah˅
loom	za˄ yoe˅
man's hat	u˅ k'o^
necklace	law˅dah
pants	la˄ di
ring	la˄ beh˅
rupee [large silver coin]	deh˅ ga˅
shirt	peh˅k'ah˅
shoulder bag	peh˅tah˅
turban	u˅ dzah˅
woman's headdress	u˅ coe˅

white	pyu˅
black	na^
red	ne˅
yellow	shui˅
blue/green	nyoe˅
beautiful	haw mui˅-eu

Health

How are (you)?	Jaw˅ sa˅ do^ mi˅-a lo˅?
(I) am well.	Jaw˅ sa˅ do^ mi˅-a.
(I) am not well.	Jaw˅ sa˅ ma˅ do^ nya.
How are (you) ill? (lit: have pain)	A˅ je˅ na˅ nya?

(My) ... hurts.	... na˅ nya.
eyes	mya^ nui^
foot	a˅ kui˅
hand	a˅ la˄
heart	nui ma si˅
stomach	u˅ ma^

(I) am sick with malaria.	Mi˅ hi˅ pya˅-ma.
(I) have diarrhoea.	U˅ ma^ yoe˅-ma.
(I) have a headache.	U˅ du˅ kaw˄ nya.
(I) have a toothache.	Seu˅ gaw˅ nya.
(My) arm is broken.	A˅ la˄ k'eh˄-i˅-ma.

When did (you) get sick?	A˅ myah neh na˅ la˅-eu˅ nya?
Have (you) taken medicine?	Ja^ g'a˅ dza˅ ma˅ lo˅?
Now (I) am taking medicine.	Nym˅-m˅ dza˅ lu˄ ma.
(I) have finished the medicine.	Dza˅ ji˅ ma˅.
(I) have not taken the medicine as yet.	Ja^ g'a˅ ma˅ ya dza˅-a si˅.
(I) had one injection of medicine.	Ja^ g'a˅ ti˅ la˄ tsaw^ ma˅.
Have (you) been (down) to the hospital?	Ho˅ ya˅-ah˅ i˅ma˅ lo˅.
(I) went, but I am not yet well.	I˅ma˅. Eh˅ k'aw˄ ma˅ ta˅ le˅-a˅ si˅.
(I) want to go (down), but I don't know the Thai language.	I˅ maw˄ mi˅-a, eh˅ k'aw˄ Tai˅ daw˅ ma˅ si˅ nya nya.
(I) have not yet gone (down).	Ma˅ i˅-a˅ si˅.

(I) am thinking of going (down) tomorrow.

Ni shaw_v i^v ma leh^v sha^v noe_v-eu ma.

(I) am not able to walk.

Ga^vma ma_v cah nya.

(I) want to bathe.

I^v cu_∧ dzui_∧ maw_∧ mi^v-a.

(You) can bathe over there.

K'oe^v paw dzui_∧ nya teh_∧-a.

Do you have soap?

Sa_v bu_v ja[∧] ma lo^v?

[They may use **sa bya**_v if from Myanmar.]

I no longer have any soap.

Nga^v sa_v bu_v ma_v pa^v ja[∧].

I want to buy (soap).

Nga^v zeu^v maw_∧ mi^v-a.

Have (you) built a toilet?

Ga^v nyi^v i^v ku[∧] tso[∧] ta_v ma lo^v.

(I) have built it.

Tso[∧] ta_v ma_v.

Do (you) want to relieve yourself?

Ga^v nyi^v i^v maw_∧ mi^v-a lo^v.

(I) want to go. [relieve myself]

I^v maw_∧ mi^v-a.

Where (is it)?

A_v geu ga^v-a.

There is a toilet below.

Ga^v nyi^v i^v ku[∧] la_∧ o[∧] paw ja[∧] meh.

(It is probable that) there is no water.

I^v cu_∧ ma_v dah_v pa_v.

I will go (to) bring water. [polite]

Nga^v i^v cu_∧ k'aw_∧-i^v ma de.

Note: Many Akha villages have no toilet. They will then say the following:

Go to the jungle.

Baw^v tsah_v i^v-eu.

Urinate.

I^vshoi shoi-eu.

AKHA

Directions & the Countryside

In the Akha language there is no one word for 'to go' or 'to come'. If you are going to a higher place or a place to the north of where you are, that is 'up'. Going to a lower place or a place to the south is 'down'. This must be known before you can select the proper verb.

come from lower	la$^\vee$-eu
go to lower	i$^\vee$-eu
come from higher	oe-eu
go to higher	le-eu

Don't come (up).	Ta$_\vee$ la$^\vee$.
Don't come (down).	Ta$_\vee$ oe.
Don't go (down).	Ta$_\vee$ i$^\vee$.
Don't go (up).	Ta$_\vee$ le.

return (down)	g'o$_\wedge$-i$^\vee$ -eu
return (up)	g'o$_\wedge$ le$^\vee$-eu
come back (up)	g'o$_\wedge$ la$^\vee$-eu
come back (down)	g'o$_\wedge$ le-eu

Is there a path?	Ga$^\vee$ma dah$^\vee$meh lo$^\vee$?
How far is the village?	Naw$_\vee$ pu a$_\vee$ mah ni ka$_\vee$-a?
It is not very far.	A$_\vee$ mah ni ma$_\vee$ ka$_\vee$ -a.
It is far.	Ga$^\vee$ mah$^\vee$ka$_\vee$-eu meh.

upper side/north	la$_\wedge$ ta$^\wedge$ paw
lower side/south	la$_\wedge$ o$^\wedge$ paw
east (sunrise side)	nah$^\vee$ma do$^\wedge$ k'eh$_\vee$ paw
west (sunset side)	nah$^\vee$ma ga k'eh$_\vee$ paw
right side	a$^\vee$ma$^\vee$paw
left side	a$^\vee$ca$^\vee$paw

In Akha there are different ways of showing that things are present or exist: animals/people, **jaw$^\vee$**; relatives, **baw**; liquid, **dah$_\vee$**, and inanimate, **ja$^\wedge$**.

There is a dog.	A˅kui˅ jaw˅meh.
I have a father.	A˅da baw ma.
There is water.	I˅cu˄ dah˅meh.
To have money.	Pyu˅ja˄ ma.
What direction should I go (up)?	A˅ geu paw ya le ta?
We don't know the path to take.	Nga ma˄ ga˅ma ma˅si˅ nya nya.
The two of us will go. [polite]	Nga nya˄ le ma de.
(We) can climb the mountain.	Gaw˅ jaw˅ da˄ le˅nya ma.
When you have climbed it, you will see the village.	Da˄ le˅na˅ pu-ah˅ya maw˅teh˄-a.
Please, the two of you, don't go today!	I˅ nah naw nya˄ ta˅ le de.
You (two) can go tomorrow.	Ni shaw˅ le nya teh˄-a.
Don't go to the right.	A˅ ma˅paw ta˅ le.
Please go to the left.	A˅ca˅paw le-aw˅ de.
Can you lead the two of us?	Naw˅nga nya˄-ah˅sheu˅ nya ma lo˅?
I am not free tomorrow.	Ni shaw˅ nga˅ma˅ dah.

bridge	law˅dzm˅
[dry] field	ya˅
[irrigated] field	deh˅ya
fire	mi˅ dza˅
moon	ba la
mountain	gaw˅ jaw˅
path	ga˅ma
rainbow	bu˅de˅le˅k'ah
river/stream	law˅ba˅
rock	k'a˅ lo
smoke	u˅ k'oe˅
sun	nah˅ ma
tree	a˅ baw˅
valley	g'a˅law˅

AKHA

Weather

The sky is clear.	M˅ mui˅-eu.
(lit: sky is good)	
It's raining.	U˅ yeh˅ yeh˅-eu.
The path is slippery.	Ga˅ ma ju˅-eu.
(I'm) cold.	Ga^-eu.
(I'm) hot.	Yaw tsa˅.
(I'm/It's) wet.	A˅-eu.

Ethnic Groups

For people, add tsaw˅ha˅ after the name; for languages, ad daw˅; for villages, add pu.

Akha	A˅ka˅
Lahu	Mui˅ seu˅
Lisu	Li˅saw˅
Shan/Northern Thai	Bi˅cm˅
Thai	Tai
Chinese	La˄bui˅
European (lit: white Indian)	Ga˅la˅ pyu˅

People

children	za˅ gu˅
friend	caw˅
baby	za˅nah˅
old people	tsaw˅maw˅
person/people	tsaw˅ha˅
boy	a˅li
girl	a˅bu˅
father	a˅ da
mother	a˅ ma
grandfather, elder male	a˅ baw˅
grandmother, elder female	a˅ pi˅
ancestors	a˅ poe˅
shaman	nyi˅pa˅

Sky God	A‸ poe‸ mi‸ yeh‸
Souls [of person]	sa‸ la‸
Spirit [ancestor, natural features]	neh‸
Spirit priest	boe‸maw‸
Village founder	dzoe‸ ma
Village headman	bu‸ seh‸

Animals

Barking deer	ci‸ha‸
Bear	k'a‸ hm‸
Bee	bya‸
Bird	a‸ji‸
Cat	a‸mi‸
Cockroach	a‸pya
Cow	maw‸ne‸
Dog	a‸ kui‸
Elephant	ya ma
Flying squirrel	ho shu‸
Gibbon	a‸myo‸ na‸

goat	ci∧ myeh∧
ground squirrel	ho ca∧ ho shaw
horse	mah∨
jungle fowl	ya nyi∨
monitor lizard	ui∨ zaw∨
monkey	a∨ myo∧
mosquito	ca∨gaw∨
otter	ui∨shm∨
panther, leopard	k'a∨ zui∨
porcupine	ho pu∨
sambar deer	k'a∨ tseh∧
sheep	yaw∨
snake	a∨law∨
tiger	k'a∨ la∨
wild boar	za∧ te∨
wildcat	a∧ hah∨

Numbers & Classifiers

Counting in Akha requires a number followed by a classifier, an in most cases they both follow the noun. For example **tsaw∨ha∨ti g'a∨**, 'person-one-human', **a∨ji∨nyi∨ maw∨**, 'bird-two-animal **a∨si∨ sm∨si∨**, 'fruit-three-round-things' and so on.

The main classifiers are:

humans	g'a∨
animals	maw∨
round things	si∨
kinds of things	je∨

The general classifier, used for things with no other classifier o when you don't know the classifier, is **hm∨**.

Sometimes the classifier is just a repetition of the word or its las syllable:

one village	**pu ti∨ pu**	one bed	**ja∧ ci∨ ti∨ ci**
	(village-one-village)		(bed-one-bed

ti_v	6	ko_∧
nyi_v	7	shi_∧
sm^v	8	yeh_∧
oe_v	9	g'oe_v
nga_v	10	tse^v

When counting alone, one and two are creaky: ti_∧ , nyi_∧. Three changes to a low tone when the classifier has a mid or high tone, as in sm_v pu, 'three villages', or sm_v maw^v, 'three animals'. Numbers from 11 to 99, apart from multiples of 10, are made with the round number plus the lower number:

11	tse^vti_∧	15	tse^vnga_v
12	tse^vnyi_∧	18	tse^vyeh_∧
25	nga_v tse^vnga_v		

Tens are formed with the lower number plus 10:

| 20 | nyi_v tse^v | 40 | oe_v tse^v |
| 30 | sm_v tse^v | 60 | ko_∧ tse^v |

Hundreds use the number ya^v, 100:

| 100 | ti_vya^v | 700 | shi_∧ ya^v |

Thousands are said one of two ways: with he_v by those from Myanmar, and with pa_v (a Thai word) by those from Thailand:

2000   nyi_v he^v or nyi_v pa^v

Ten thousand is meu^v and 100,000 is seh. Both of these are borrowed from Thai or related languages. Some examples follow.

1998	ti_v pa^v g'oe_vya^v g'oe_vtse^v yeh_∧ k'o_∧
235 animals	nyi_vya^v sm_vtse^vnga_vmaw^v
57 people	nga_vtse^v shi_∧ g'a_v

Time Words

Some time words are also used as classifiers after numbers, when counting time:

day	nah
night	mi˅
four nights	oe˅ mi˅
year	k'oʌ
three years	sm˅k'oʌ

but others, like **bala**, 'month', are not:

two months	bala nyi˅si˅
yesterday	mi˅ nah
today	i˅ nah
tomorrow	ni shaw˅
day after tomorrow	sa˅ peh˅
now	nym˅-m˅
this morning [said in morning]	nym˅ shaw˅
this morning [said in afternoon]	mi˅ shaw˅
this evening [said in evening]	nym˅ ciʌ
this evening [said in morning]	a˅ no ciʌ

AKHA

Just two or three days.	Nyi˅ nah sm˅ nah tehʌ-a si˅.
It has been one month.	Ba la ti˅ si˅ byah la˅ ma˅.
It is probably about one or two years.	Ti˅ k'oʌ nyi˅ k'oʌ keuʌ la˅-eu˅ du˅.

CULTURE & LOCATIONS

The Lisu are a group of some 950,000 people; about 650,000 live along the western borders of Yunnan in China, with about 250,000 in the far north of Myanmar, several thousand in north-eastern India, and about 35,000 in Thailand. Almost all of those in Thailand have come from the southernmost Lisu areas in China over the last 50 years, and speak a dialect of Lisu heavily influenced by Yunnanese Chinese. This dialect is different from the 'standard' Lisu used in China and Myanmar.

Most Lisu in Thailand live in the mountains in relatively remote locations; some are in mixed villages with Red Lahu in Chiang Rai province or in areas adjacent to Lahu settlements elsewhere, and many Lisu can speak some Lahu as well as Yunnanese Chinese, Northern Thai and some Thai. Some of the fathers and grandfathers in these Lisu families are Chinese, former KMT (Nationalist) soldiers, who married Lisu women.

Traditional Lisu religion focuses on three or four shrines under a large tree in a fenced area above each village, where the guardian spirits are regularly feted, and on an altar for the ancestors at the back of each house. Females should not enter the fenced area, and no guest should touch any shrines. Religion and traditional culture are not as important factors in Lisu life as they are for the Lahu, Akha, or other related groups of Thailand. Still important are family, kinship and clan ties.

Some Lisu houses are built on posts raised above the ground, using available local materials (wood, bamboo, thatch) or more recently boards and metal roofing sheets. Others are built on the ground like Chinese houses, reflecting the mixed origin of the Lisu in Thailand. The porch and door are at the downhill end of the house, aligned with the ancestral altar at the uphill end. Guests should not enter the family bedrooms at the back, and should not sleep with their head towards the fire.

Lisu in Thailand

LISU

Authority figures in a Lisu village include the headman and the village priest. Most guests will be invited to stay in the headman's house unless they know someone else in the village or the headman already has many guests.

The most interesting celebrations in a Lisu village are the New Year (approximately the same time as Chinese New Year, but locally determined by the village priest) and weddings; both involve ceremonies, feasting, and a lot of drinking. For the New Year the centre of activities is the New Year tree, specially cut and brought into the village. People in their best clothes and decked out in all their silver dance and sing for several days and nights, around it and elsewhere in the village.

LISU

In a wedding, the bride's family receives a large amount of silver or money from the groom's; poor Lisu men may have trouble acquiring a Lisu wife. Weddings involve a lot of feasting and singing. Another colourful part of Lisu life is courtship; groups of young men travel around dressed in their best clothes and carrying their instruments, playing and singing with the unmarried girls, mostly in the evenings and usually not in their own village. Some of their instruments are of Chinese origin, such as the two-string lute; others are shared with other hill tribe groups, such as the gourd reed-organ, bamboo flute and jew's-harp.

Lisu make very attractive shoulder bags, basically off-white with vertical red stripes; fancier bags have more colours in narrow horizontal strips by the opening, red or multicoloured tassels at the sides and bottom, and sometimes even silver ornaments are sewn on. Items of clothing including shoulder bags are made for sale, and Lisu silversmiths also make new jewellery in traditional styles, sometimes using silver but more often white metal. The supply of silver coins previously used for jewellery and traditional payments is running out, with Thai currency now widely used instead.

LISU

Changes in dress styles have been frequent and substantial among Lisu in different areas. The far northern Lisu in China and Myanmar wear completely different clothes from those in Thailand. In Thailand, Lisu women wear long coats which fold across the chest; at the top are narrow strips of red, white, yellow and other coloured cloth in a wide arc centred around the neck. Sleeves are usually red, and the body is in blue or blue-green. Under this, short black trousers and red leggings with blue hems are worn. The women's turban is flat and black, ornamented with brightly coloured strings. On festive occasions the family silver is dug up; small round silver buttons and bells are sewn on to the front of the coat, and elaborate silver necklaces and earrings are worn above them. For everyday wear, the turban is often just a white towel and silver is nowhere to be seen.

Thailand Lisu men wear baggy blue or blue-green Shan style trousers, a black shirt and a small white turban; again, on festive occasions silver buttons and bells are sewn on to the front of the shirt, and ornamental strips of red or other brightly coloured string or cloth are added to the bottom of the shirt and turban. Nowadays the turban may be replaced by a towel and the Lisu shirt by a T-shirt for everyday wear.

The first Lisu village to be established in Thailand (in 1918) is at Doi Chang, south-west of Chiang Rai. This village is frequently visited; other readily accessible villages are all along the north of Thailand, along the Kok River and to its north in Chiang Rai, also in northern Chiang Mai and Mae Hong Son provinces. Smaller numbers have recently moved south to western Tak and Kampaengphet provinces.

SOUNDS

There are substantial dialect differences within Lisu; the forms given here are those used in Thailand. In the writing system shown here, the values of the letters differ from those of the other four languages in this book, but mainly correspond to the Chinese pinyin system.

LISU

Vowels

The vowels are also fairly numerous; they include i, ei and ai which are like the vowels in 'be', 'bait' and 'bat', u which is actually pronounced 'vu'; also o and two vowels similar to 'u' and 'o' but said with the lips spread and both indicated by e in the writing system. Absent from the writing in China but widespread in Lisu dialects are two vowels like the German 'ü' and 'ö', or French 'u' and 'eu': said like 'i' and 'e' but with the lips rounded. These Lisu vowels are written oi.

Consonants

There are the following voiceless unaspirated sounds: b, d, z (ts), j (ch) and g. Aspirated sounds are p, t, c (hts), q (hch) and k. For more information on how to pronounce aspirated and unaspirated sounds, see the Introduction, page 15.

Voiced sounds, like English 'b', 'd' and 'g' in 'big', 'dig' and 'gig', are bb, dd, zz (dz), jj and gg. M, n, ng, f, s, sh, v, y, w, l and r are the same as in English. The Lisu h represents either an English-like 'h' sound, a sound like the Scots 'ch' in 'loch', or a nasal 'h' sound; this writing system doesn't separate these three forms of 'h'. The 'z' sound is written as ss, and a voiced sound like the French 'r' or Lahu g' is written as rr. There are a few combinations of consonants at the beginning of the word; these include b, p, bb, m, n and hl followed by a medial 'y' sound, then written as -i-; and g, k, gg and ng followed by a 'w' sound, written as -u-.

Tones

Lisu has six tones, two of which involve constriction of the voice and four of which do not. The writing shows five of these tones with a consonant following the vowel. For example, the following are six different words in Lisu:

see	mo
old	mot
to aim/millstone	mol
tattoo	moq

| high | mox |
| weed/to weed | mor |

No consonant after the vowel indicates the mid tone. The following t indicates a low tone and following l shows a high tone. The q represents a rising tone, x is for a mid tone said with a creaky sound, and r represents a low, short tone with a creaky sound or cut off with a glottal stop.

THE LANGUAGE

The variety of Lisu spoken in Thailand is a simplified version of the 'standard' variety on which the writing is based. There are several competing Lisu writing systems, including one widely used by Christian Lisu in Myanmar and China and one developed in China in the 1950s. The former, usually called the Fraser script, uses upper case Roman letters, upside down as well as normal, for consonants and vowels; and punctuation marks for tones. The latter, the new script, uses only Roman letters; this is used here. Very few Lisu in Thailand are literate in Lisu, but with the spread of education some are becoming literate in Thai.

Forming Sentences

As in Lahu and Akha, the verb of the sentence usually comes after all the nouns. For example, Ngua zza zzat, 'I rice eat', not 'I eat rice'. Lisu in Thailand is even less complex than Lahu or Akha, because there are fewer grammatical markers. It has freer grammar in that sentences can be rearranged, but the basic and most frequent pattern is verb-final.

Like most languages of the area, Lisu has many modal elements that come before, or more often after, the main verb; for example dda, 'may'. These can be piled up after the verb, as English sometimes piles them up before the verb: Nu la li jjuaq nga (you come must have be-the-case), 'You must come/You may have to come'. Some other frequent modals include wax, also 'must', and ko 'can'.

As in other related languages, Lisu needs an extra classifier after every number; the number comes after the noun being counted, as in cossat tit yo (person-one-classifier), 'one person'. There are many classifiers, but the most frequently needed are yo for people and kaq for animals; for most other things the general classifier ma may be used.

Most expressions of time, place and so on, come at the beginning of the sentence, or before the verb, as in Nilmei ngua zza zzat, 'Today I eat rice'. The negative comes immediately before the verb, as in Nilmei ngua zza ma zzat, 'Today I don't eat rice'.

Pronouns

Lisu tends to leave out pronouns where it's already obvious who is doing what, but for clarity you can always put them in. They are ngua, 'I'; nu , 'you'; yil, 'he/she/it'; the plurals may be expressed by the singular form, or for emphasis the plural forms ngua nut, 'you and I'; nu wat, 'you' (plural); and yil wat, 'they' are available. The possessor, pronoun or other noun, precedes the item possessed: ngua hin, 'my house'; Asa hin, 'Asa's house'. There's no other marking on the possessor; thus, for example, 'I', 'me' and 'my' are all just ngua.

Questions

Questions with a 'yes' or 'no' answer are asked by repeating the verb, with a negative in between, effectively providing the two alternative answers: Nu zza zzat mat zzat? (you rice eat not eat), 'Do you eat rice?'. Questions requiring a more substantial answer have a question word such as ali 'which', for example Ali ma zza zzat? 'Who eats rice?' (which classifier rice eat). Note that the words are in the same order in statements and questions, unlike most European languages; question words aren't necessarily first in the sentence.

To ask what something is called, indicate it and ask Tei ma ali bbaix?, 'What is this called?' – but be aware that Lisu people don't usually point at things with one finger, instead using a gesture pointing the chin; so you may instead be given the word for 'finger', lair ni.

Orders and requests can be made directly, as in Nu zza zzat la! (you rice eat come), 'You come and eat', or more politely as a question such as Nu la ma la? 'Are you coming?'; more politely still by using a modal such as ddạ 'can': Nu la dda mat dda? (you come can not can), 'Can you come?'; or even more politely by asking whether someone said that they would do something: Nu la nga bbaix? (you come be-the-case say), 'Did you say it's correct that you are coming?'.

<table>
<tr><td colspan="2">Question Words</td></tr>
</table>

who?	at ma
what?	al shit
when?	al tait
where?	al lal
how much?	a miai ci
how many? [+ classifier]	a mia
which ...?	a li ...
why?	al shit wol ni

To Be

There is no verb like 'to be' in sentences such as Yit mux-a, 'He is tall', because the adjective itself functions as the verb. However for emphasis one may end these or almost any other positive sentence with nga, 'be the case, be correct, be true', which is usually optional but is the closest thing to a verb 'to be' that Lisu has. 'Yes' can also be nga or ngot. 'No' is Mat nga or hel. When you wish to equate two nouns, the sentence usually ends with the same nga: Ngua mi Asa nga, 'My name is Asa'. If you want to say that something exists or you have it, use the verb jjuaq alone as in Mat jjuaq, 'There isn't any' or '(I) haven't got any' or with other words as in Ajjaix jjuaq mat jjuaq, ngua tit ket ddo (water have not have, I one bit drink), 'Do (you) have water, I'll drink a bit?'. Thus the verb 'to be' is expressed in a number of different ways or not at all, depending on the type of sentence and degree of emphasis.

References

In 1974 Pacific Linguistics at the Australian National University in Canberra, Australia published a grammar of Thailand Lisu by Edward R. Hope, but this is now out of print. In 1994 the same publisher produced a useful Lisu-English and English-Lisu dictionary by David Bradley which describes the northernmost dialect as spoken in China; this is somewhat different from the Lisu spoken in Thailand. By late 1998 the same author will finish a new Thailand Lisu-English dictionary, and there's a long-term project to prepare a dictionary for all of the varieties of Lisu. For those who read French, in 1994 Gallimard published a collection of translations of Lisu stories with an excellent introduction by William Dessaint and Avòunado Ngwâza, Au Sud des Nuages.

WORDS & PHRASES
Greetings & Civilities

What is it?	Ali nga?

The above is the usual greeting; the following are three possible answers:

(I) am very busy now.	Tei zil mit atkel cat niaq nga.
	(lit: this time work very busy able be)
(I) don't have much to do.	Alshit lil mat yi niaq.
	(lit: what all not do able)
(I) don't have much on.	Atdor nat niaq nga.
	(lit: this side able be)
Where are you going?	Nu ala jjei nga?
	(lit: you where go be)
I am going to the village.	Ngua zeilzi jjei nga.
	(lit: I village go be)

I am going to wash myself.	Ngua ggoddeit cit jjei.
	(lit: I body wash go)
I am going home.	Ngua hin kut jjei.
	(lit: I home to go)

Where have you come from?	Nu al lal jox la nga?
	(lit: you where out-of come be)
Where is your home/house?	Nu hin ala ddaq-a?
I have come from the market.	Ngua ga-i zir jox la.
I have come for a visit.	Ngua chual la.

Have you eaten?	Nu zza zzat mat zzat?
I have eaten.	Ngua zza zzat o.
I have not eaten yet.	Ngua zza mat zzat sir.

Come inside the house.	Hiku a nat la.
Sit down.	Niq dal jaq-a.
Drink tea.	Catyi ddo.
Drink water.	Ajjaix ddo.

Thank you.	Xual mu wa; Atkel bboxmu
	or Dut zoil.

Good, very good!	Nga, nga qar!
(I) want to go.	Lat jjei ddor wa.
[said by person who is about to leave]	
Until later.	Nat sir.
[said by person staying or person going]	
Go slowly.	Assa assa jjei.
[said by person staying]	

YOU'RE WELCOME!

The phrase Olli tat bbaix! – You're welcome! – has a literal meaning of 'Don't say that!'.

LISU

WHICH LANGUAGE?

I don't understand.	Ngua na naq mat meir.
Please say that again.	Ame tit to bbaix.
Can you speak ...?	Nu ... tei gul mat gul?
Chinese	Het ngot
Thai	Tai ngot
Burmese	Lot mieit ngot
English	Ang kix ngot

Small Talk

What is your name?	Nu imi ali nga?
My name is ...	Ngua mi ... nga.
Where do you come from?	Nu agua jo la nga?
I come from ...	Ngua ... gua jo la nga.
Thailand	Ta-i met
Myanmar	Lot mieit met
China	Het met
Do you have a wife?	Nu ssatme hua ggu wai?
Do you have a husband?	Nu ssatggu hiaq wai?
I am not married yet.	Ngua hi mat hua heit.
How many brothers and sisters do you have?	Nu kolko cil cil nixssat nixmax amia yo niaq?
Do you have children?	Nu ssatnei niaq mat niaq?
I don't have any.	Mat jjuaq.
I have ...	Ngut ... niaq nga.
two children	ssatnei nit yo
one older brother	kolko tit yo
three older sisters	jiljil sa yo
four younger brothers	nixssat li yo
five younger sisters	nixmax nguat yo

LISU

Accommodation & Meals

May I sleep in your house?	Ngua nu hinkut a eirdal dda mat dda?
Can I stay in your house one night?	Ngua nu hi tit metkel nat mat dda?
(You) may.	Dda nga.
How much is a car to the market?	Tei gua jo ga-i zirgua chi tait lox ge pet amia nga?
A car is ... 20 baht	Lox ge pet ... nici bbar
Where shall I put my things?	Ngua ex ma agua nat bbaix?
Put it there.	Ta ge dal.

Do you have (a) ...?   Nu ... jjuaq mat jjuaq?
    blanket   yiq bbe
    flashlight (torch)   ma ta
    lamp   lail wa
    mat   tat por or siqzir
    mattress   pal gol
    mosquito net   zal pot
    pillow   wol gor lo
    soap   cat biax

Can you lend me ...?   Nu ngua dail ... tit ma ngol
        la dda ma dda?

LISU

I will buy ...   Ngua ... vu.
   batteries (flashlight)   ma ta sil
   (chicken) eggs   alyal fu
   fish   nguat
   pork   vair huat
   one chicken   alyal tit ma

Will (you) give me ...?   Nu ngua dail ... get mat get?
   banana   nga ma sil
   chopsticks   al jju
   a teacup   lux ge
   a dish   bbaix
   fruit   siq sit
   hot water   yi luei
   a (small) knife   al tat (leir)
   mango   mut mu
   salt   catbbo
   a spoon   ssiq ggu
   a stool   bat deq

How much will you   ... amia vut nga?
sell ... for?
   one (chicken) egg   alyal fu tit ma
   one animal   tit kaq
   one (thing)   tit ma

Can you cook a bit   Ngua dail ... atdil jal ggot la
of ... for me?   dda mat dda?
   soup   ot piat yi
   (cooked) rice   zza
   pork   vair xuat
   chicken   al yal xuat
   vegetables   wot piat
   pumpkin   al poit
   eggplant   ggua sil
   beans   al nor
   jackfruit   al nil her ma
   yam   bbit

LISU

(I) am hungry.	Zza heir mer-a.
(I) am thirsty.	Ajjaix ser-a.
(I) am full.	Pa bbo zzat.
or	Zzat bbo le-o.
Are (you) full yet?	Zzat bbo wa?
Drink liquor!	Zzi ddo!
I don't eat chillies.	Ngua laqzir mat zzat.
Do you have salt?	Nu catbbo jjuaq mat jjuaq?
(This is) delicious!	Atkel zzat mi!
Do (you) smoke tobacco?	Nu yiqgul chir mat chir?
I don't smoke.	Ngua mat chir.
I want to smoke tobacco.	Ngua yiqgul chir shix-a.
I don't smoke opium.	Ngua yatpil mat chir.
Are you tired?	Nu mat or he?
Do you want to sleep?	Nu eir dal mat dal?
(I) am very sleepy.	Yir mex lei-a.
Lie down.	Yir dal.

Traditional Life & Crafts

The non-Christian Lisu have a sabbath or rest day every 14 days at the moon phases. Their main festival corresponds to the Chinese New Year and is celebrated with music, feasting and drinking, as are weddings; people also dig up their jewellery and wear their best clothes at these times. In each traditional village there is a spirit grove at the top of the village, where the sky god and other main gods are propitiated; each house also has its ancestor altar at the back of the house.

New Year	kot shit
rice cake	nal put
[special for New Year, made of pounded sticky rice]	
Sky God [main god]	Yil ddat ma
Sky Goddess	Mi six max
Christian God	Wu sax

LISU

village priest	memex
non-Christian spirit	net
shaman/traditional doctor	net pat
Lisu customs	Lisu lit
sabbath	zil ni
ancestor altar	daq bbiar
full moon	habba ci lul
waning moon	habba pu
waxing moon	habba naix
'banjo'	ci bbe or toiq
gourd reed-organ	fut luq
jew's-harp	max go
drum	kut
gong	ma
flute	jit
loom	yar nil yat max

Shopping

Will you buy a shoulder bag?	Nu lair bbia vo mat vo?
How much is the shoulder bag?	Lair bbia yit pet amia nga?
How much will you give?	Nu amia gget?
The price is too expensive!	Yil pet got zir lei-u!
It's not too expensive.	Tei kel mat goil.

LISU

I want to buy (a) ...	Ngua ... vo shix-a.
belt	jjit heq
bracelet	lair jjux
button	neit zix
leggings	ci jjux
necklace	na koq or lix wot
pants	mi ci
pipe	ggor ggor
purse	lair shal
ring	lair ni keq
rupee [large silver coin]	yat cit
shirt	bboi cit
shoulder bag	lair bbia
silver buckle	beix ket
white	pu
black	naix
red	shit
	[in China and Myanmar: nit]
yellow	shix
blue/green	niq qir
beautiful	bbi-a
not beautiful	mat bbi
very beautiful	akhel bbi-a

Health

wash one's hands	lairpaiq cit-a
wash one's body	ggoddeit cit-a
I am going to the bathroom.	ngua neshi-a rrei-a
	(lit: go outdoors)
I am a bit sick.	Ngua ggaoxddeit adil na.
I have indigestion.	Ngua cut nol.
I have malaria.	Ngua qahe na-a.
I have a sore throat.	Ngua wo qi jul-a.
I have diarrhoea.	Ngua heir ma ggat.

LISU

My ... hurts.	Ngua ... na.
ear	nal bo
eyes	myax sil
head	wol vet
heart	niq ma
leg/foot	ci paiq
stomach	heir ma
tooth	sil ci

My lower back is sore.	Ngua jjit jil na-a.
My arm is broken.	Ngua lairpaiq shil li wa.
I am menstruating.	Ngua ha bba jo lo.

Do you have medicine?	Nu niacir jjuaq mat jjuaq?
Go and get a doctor!	Nu niacir sipat hua jjei.
Can you carry me?	Nu ngua dail mai jji?

Directions & the Countryside

Lisu village	Lisu zeil zi
Lahu village	Lat heq zeilzi
Akha village	Atkat zeilzi
car/bus	lox

Which direction?	Ali tit fa?
How do I go to ...?	... ali jjei?
Is the path good?	Zzaggu sa ma sa?
The path is not so good.	Zzaggu atkel mat sa.
Not very far.	Atkel mat rret.

Can a car go there?	Lox ci la wa?
Will you come with me?	Nu ngua gel nia tit da jjei dda mat dda?
Can you take me there by car?	Nu ngua dail lox gua jol hot fu yi bbaix?
Can you carry my things?	Nu ngua ex mai jjua bbaix?
How much money should I give you?	Ngua nu dail pu amia gget lai bbaix?

Go ...	... jjei.
straight	luluq
right side	lair yax
left side	lair rrel
above	gel zil shi
below	wo boil shi
in front	mit tait shi
behind	gal nial shi
uphill	ggar bol shi
downhill	wur bol shi

to go	jjei-a
[away from where speaker is now]	
to come	la-a
[towards where speaker is now]	
to go up	daix-a
to go down	rair-a

LISU

bridge	ggot jjoi
[unirrigated, sloping] field	ha mi
[irrigated, flat] field	ddei mi
fire	al dol
moon	ha bba
mountain	wat zzit
path	zza ggu
river/stream	yi jja lu
rock	lal ci
smoke	met kut
sun	mit mix
tree	siq zzi
valley	lu kut
waterfall	rral yi qeiq

Weather

The sun is shining.	Met ca ca-a.
It's raining.	Met ha lix-a.
It's hailing.	Wat sit cei-a.
The path is slippery.	Zza ggu nia ziq loit-a.
It's muddy.	Lalbal hoi-a.
(I'm) cold.	Jjat-a.
(I'm) hot.	Ca-a.
(I'm/It's) wet.	Par liei-a.

Ethnic Groups

[person: add co after the name; village: add zeil zi]

Lisu	Li su
Lahu	Lat heq
Akha	At kat
Meo (Mong)	Miao zi
Yao (Mien)	Yar ja
Shan	Bbex yi
Northern Thai	Go lo
Thai	Ta-i
Chinese	Het pat

Karen   Yal gel lel
Kachin   Qut pat

People

person	co
friend	cot paiq
man	co bal ssat
woman	ssat me-ar
young unmarried man	ssat met lail
young unmarried woman	ssat ggu lail
old man	co mot
old woman	alyait
headman	hua to pat
baby	co shir ssat

LISU

SOME USEFUL WORDS

to sell	vut-a
to buy	vo-a
to give	gget-a
to take	ssu-a
to dance	ggua qeiq-a
to sing	mut gguat gguax
to be happy	niq ma ho-a
to be sad	niq ma cit-a
to marry (join hands)	lairpaiq zal
to divorce	haq lair ho-a
to remember	jil mex-a
to forget	mi lei-a
quickly	ail mil
slowly	a ssa a ssa
country/nation	met
market	ga-i zir
town	kaq dat ma
jungle	li ca mi
bicycle	beiq lox
silver	pu
gold	shix
this	te
that	ggo
here	ta

Animals

barking deer [small deer]	qi
bear	wo
bee	bbiat
bird	niaq
cat	a niaq zi
cattle	al nit
dog	al nat

LISU

elephant	ha ma
gibbon	myoir wat lat
horse	al mot
jungle fowl	al yal gol
leech	veir
louse	he
monkey	jaq myoir
porcupine	al bux
rat	al pet
cockroach	bbeit sal max
sambar deer [large deer]	qeiq
snake	fu
squirrel	al bbeit
tiger	lat ma
water buffalo	al ngar
wild boar	al vair til

Numbers & Classifiers

Counting in Lisu requires a classifier after the number; these two follow the noun, so Lisu tit yo, 'one Lisu' is literally 'Lisu-one-human'. The common classifier is ma. With numbers ending in a zero, the classifier isn't needed. As seen in examples above, animals are better counted with kaq, people with yo, fruit or small round things with sit, and Thai money (Baht) with bar instead of ma.

1	tit ma	6	qur ma
2	nit ma	7	shit ma
3	sa ma	8	her ma
4	li ma	9	gux ma
5	nguat ma	10	tit ci (lit: 1,10)

LISU

The round numbers are made with the number plus the number 10, ci:

30	sa ci (lit: 3,10)	90	gux ci (lit: 9,10)

The hundreds are similarly combined from the number plus 100, hi; thousands are the number plus 1000, du, and tens of thousands are the number plus 10,000, met:

100	tit hia	500	nguat hia
2000	nit du	10,000	tit met

Combinations go from largest to smallest:

1998	tit du gux hia kux ci her niq
555	nguat hia nguat ci nguat ma
35	sa ci nguat ma

Time Words

Basic time words can also be used as classifiers:

day	ni	month	ha bba
10 days	ci ni	four months	li ha bba
night	hia		

There are two words for 'year'; kor and niq; the former is a traditional word and a usual classifier but the latter is also used.

six years	qor niq
yesterday	at mei
today	nil mei
tomorrow	sal nair
day after tomorrow	wa ni
this morning	nil nair
this evening	nil met ket

LISU

CULTURE, SUBGROUPS & LOCATIONS

The Mong – who are known as Miao in Chinese, as Meo in Vietnamese, and as Maew in Thai and Lao – are a group of nearly ten million people who originated in southwestern China but have been migrating southwestwards for a millenium or more under pressure from the expanding Chinese. Over 8.5 million still live in various southwestern provinces of China, especially Guizhou but also Yunnan, Guangxi, Hunan and Sichuan. There's enormous diversity within this group in China, to the extent that it may be impossible for them to understand each other. There are over 600,000 in Vietnam, over a quarter of a million in Laos, about 120,000 in Thailand, about 100,000 refugees from Laos living in western countries and a few in Myanmar. All those outside China and over a million of those in Yunnan and parts of western Guizhou in China speak dialects quite similar to the one given here.

They started to arrive in Thailand in the late 19th century, with the flow gradually increasing, especially after the change of government in Laos in 1975. Because many of the Mong in Laos were associated with the army of the Mong General Vang Pao who was funded by the American CIA, several hundred thousand fled to Thailand in the mid to late 1970s. Most of these have now migrated to western countries, especially the US (85,000) and France (10,000) with smaller numbers in Canada and Australia, or been repatriated to Laos; a few managed to stay in Thailand with those Mong already in the country before 1975.

Of the Mong in Thailand the majority belong to the subgroup known as Green Mong (Moob Ntsuab). The other subgroup represented is the White Hmong (Hmood Dawb). Although these are the names that the Mong themselves prefer, they are also known collectively as Miao (from Chinese) or Meo (from Thai and Lao). Furthermore, the Green Mong (Moob

MONG

Mong (Meo) in Thailand

MYANMAR

LAOS

Chiang Rai

Mae Hong Song

Phayao

Chiang Mai

Nan

Lamphun

Lampang

Phrae

Uttaradit

Loei

Tak

Sukhotai

Phitsanulok

Phetchabun

Kamphaeng Phet

Phichit

Nakhon Sawan

Uthai Thani

THAILAND

ANDAMAN SEA

Suphan Buri

Kanchanaburi

BANGKOK

Ratchaburi

Bight of Bangkok

Phetchaburi

0   100   200 km

Ntsuab) are called 'Blue Meo' by the Thai. The word ntsuab could be translated as either 'green' or '(dark) blue', but the Mong think of blue as the colour of sickness and death; green is the colour of life, and so is obviously the preferred translation. Green Mong are also rather derogatorily nicknamed 'Striped Hmong' (Hmoob Leej) by the White Hmong, because of the horizontal stripes on the women's skirts.

MONG

Traditional Mong settlements are nearly always found at the highest altitudes: at least 1000 metres and sometimes over 1200. Villages are really just small clusters of hamlets, usually without any central building, such as a temple, for common use. Very few Mong in Thailand have been converted to Buddhism or Christianity. The great majority follow traditional animist beliefs. Ceremonies such as the propitiation of spirits, or the calling of the wandering souls of the sick, are led by a shaman, who comes to the home of the family concerned. In the case of sickness or some other malady, a household, or even a whole village, may be declared 'off-limits' to visitors for a couple of days. This is clearly signalled, near the entrance, by a waist-high pole, topped with a disc woven from bamboo, and some green leaves.

At all other times the Mong are most welcoming towards visitors. The village headman is primarily responsible for hospitality. The best time of all to visit is just before and during the New Year festivities, usually held around the end of November, but sometimes as late as early January, depending on the time of the harvest. Mong visit each other at this time too, so accommodation will be a bit tight. Leading up to the New Year there's less work done in the fields, and much activity in the village, finishing off new clothing (which may have been all year in the making), slaughtering the New Year's pig, and preparing other special food. The festivities include games like spinning the top, a kind of badminton, and also a courting game where young men and women throw colourful cloth balls to one another, signalling interest by favouring one particular partner. Weddings often occur at this time and traditional music is also a feature.

MONG

Houses are made of wood, with thatched or shingle roofs. Green Mong houses have only one door, which faces downhill. White Hmong have a second door, generally on the side to the left of the downhill door. It's best to use this second door when visiting a White Hmong house, as the downhill door may be reserved for religious ceremonies. The family bedrooms are on the left side of the downhill door, and the guest bed to the right. The main fireplace, around which everyone gathers to chat, is not far from the entrance. There's a smaller clay fireplace, for cooking pig's food and so on, towards the uphill side of the house, and a raised altar, which is always opposite the downhill door.

Around the walls are various storage shelves, and there is also a raised platform for drying food-stuffs, reached by a ladder which only certain members of the household are permitted to ascend.

It is possible to tell which subgroup a Mong person belongs to by their traditional cloth-ing. Green Mong women wear dark blue pleated skirts with a batik de-sign, overlaid with stripes of colourful appliqué and embroidery. This is worn with a narrow black and blue 'apron' and a black shirt which s often embroidered. The hair is tied in a chignon, with little or no decoration. White Hmong now rarely wear their traditional white pleated skirts with black leggings. Dark baggy trousers are more common, with an embroidered 'apron' both front and back. The chignon may be covered by a black turban or embroidered hat. Shirts are colourfully embroidered, as are the 'sailor collars' at the back. These collars are also worn by Green Mong women, but are smaller, with the decorated side concealed. All the men wear black shirts with embroidered edges and baggy black trousers. The Green Mong have an extremely long crotch to these trousers, and also wear a black toque decorated with embroidery and pompoms. All Mong, men and women, wear long sashes and, on ceremonial occasions, heavy silver necklaces and coin belts.

Paaj-ntaub ('flower cloth') is the handicraft for which the Mong are best known. Green Mong women are particularly skilled in batik, used as a base for skirts and baby-carriers, and White Hmong women specialise in reverse appliqué work; all do exquisite cross-stitch. Non-traditional paaj-ntaub items, made particularly in refugee camps, include cushion, pillow and quilt covers, table runners and wall hangings. The latter are often embroidered in a narrative style, depicting legends, daily life, or flight from war. If the camps are not accessible, work from them is on sale in the Night Bazaar, Chiang Mai, or in the nearby village of Doi Pui.

Mong settlements are to be found in many provinces in Northern Thailand, the majority in Chiang Mai, Tak and Chiang Rai (more White Hmong here than in other areas). There are also some villages in Phrae, Lampang, Phayao, Kamphaeng Phet, Mae Hong Son, Sukhothai, Phitsanulok, and Loei, and quite a number in Phetchaburi (mostly refugees from previous conflict within Thailand). Of course, most of the organised treks take place in Chiang Mai. Tak, and particularly Chiang Rai provinces, would be more suitable for those who want to strike out alone. Villages sometimes move due to soil exhaustion, so check that maps and information are really up to date.

MONG

References

For more information about Mong culture and daily life, see *Migrants of the Mountains* by William Geddes (Oxford: Clarendon Press, 1976) or the book by Paul & Elaine Lewis noted in the introduction.

SOUNDS
Vowels

The simple vowels in Green Mong are:

a   as in 'father'
e   as in 'obey' (but without the 'i' offglide at the end)
i   as in 'machine'
o   as in British/American English 'hot'
u   as in 'lunar'
w   which sounds like the first vowel in 'er ...', said with very spread, relaxed lips.

The vowel clusters are:

ai   which sounds like a plus i, as in 'aisle'
ao   which is a plus o
aw   which is a plus w
au   which is a plus u, as in '(Nikki) Lauda'
ua   which is u plus a.

There are quite a number of words in which au and ua can be used interchangeably, for example rau/rua which means 'to' or 'for'. The 'nasalised' vowels are pronounced like a simple vowel, plus the 'ng' of 'sing'. However, they can't be written with a vowel plus 'ng', because the writing system uses the position after the vowel in each syllable to indicate the tone. So, instead, the vowel symbol is doubled. Aa sounds like the last part of 'sung'; ee varies quite a bit, from the 'eng' sound of 'strength' to the 'ing' sound of 'England'; and oo sounds like the last part of British/Australian English 'song'.

Consonants

The difference between pairs of sounds like ph and p, plh, th and t, dlh and dl, and th, tsh and ts, rh and r, kh and k, qh and q may require a bit of practice to master. The first of each of these pairs is said with a strong puff of air, just like the sounds at the beginning of English 'pat', 'plait', 'tart', 'cat'. The second of each pair has no puff of air, like the sounds after the 's' in English 'spat', 'splat', 'start', 'scat'. These second ones really sound a lot more like a weak version of English 'b', 'bl', 'd' and 'g', rather than English 'p', 'pl', 'd' and 'k' at the beginning of a word.

There is another pair, l and hl, which are related to each other in a slightly different way. The l is pronounced just as in English. For hl, put your tongue in the same position as for l, and just breathe out strongly, so that the air rushes out over the sides of your tongue. The h by itself is generally just like the English 'h', but a few speakers pronounce it more like the English 'f'. The sounds dl (as in 'fiddler') and dlh ('tl' with a puff of air, as in 'butler') are sometimes pronounced, and written, kl (as in 'back lane') and klh (as in 'clown') respectively. The sounds q and qh aren't at all like 'q' in English. They're like the English 'k', but pronounced much farther back. Open your mouth as wide as you can and make the sound a crow makes: 'kaa, kaa'.

The Mong letter x, which appears by itself as well as in combinations like tx and txh, is quite similar to an English 's' said with just a bit of a lisp: put your tongue just behind your front teeth and say 's', 'ts', etc. Well, if the Mong x is like English 's', what is Mong s like? By itself it's pronounced like the 'sh' in 'shout'. The combinations ts and tsh are like the first sounds in 'judge' and 'church' respectively. The Mong z is like the 's' in 'treasure', not like the 'z' in 'zebra'.

The sound symbolised by xy is, unfortunately, not just a combination of Mong x plus 'y'. It's much more like the sound of the friction you get when you laugh 'he-he-he'. The letters c and ch are formed from this sound, xy, with a 't' sound in front of it – a 't' pronounced with the tongue pushed right forward behind the front teeth, so that not just the tip, but also the blade, is touching the teeth. So c and ch, sound a bit like the first sounds in 'jeep' and 'cheese' respectively, but with the tongue starting much farther forward.

Mong t and th are also pronounced with the tongue forward behind the teeth, but only the tongue tip, not the blade, touches the teeth for these sounds. The consonants r and rh, on the other hand, are made by curling the tongue right up to the back of the gum ridge. They sound just like the 'dr' and 'tr' in 'drain' and 'train'. There are some Green Mong speakers, however, who don't make a distinction between r and ts (likewise, between rh and tsh, etc).

Nearly all of the pairs of sounds noted above also occur with the letter n before them. So you get nt, like the 'nd' in 'under', and nth, like the 'nt' in winter', etc. However, the n in np/nph and npl/nplh is pronounced 'm', just as we might sometimes say the 'n' in 'input'. Likewise, the n in nk/nkh is like English 'ng' (as in 'sing'), like the 'n' might sound in 'ingratitude' or 'incredible'. There's also a consonant ny, as the 'ny' in 'canyon'.

Tones

Every word in Green Mong has its own tone. If you put the wrong vowel or consonant in a word, you will either make a word which means something different, or a nonsense word; the same applies if you use the wrong tone.

Tones in Mong are symbolised by a consonant symbol at the end of the syllable. This doesn't mean that the tone is something which is said after the vowel; the symbol actually tells you how the vowel is said.

The tone symbols and their pronunciations are as follows:

unmarked	mid, level pitch
b	high, level pitch (think of the English word 'balance' to help you remember)
j	starts high and falls in pitch (think of 'jump')
g	starts not so high and falls with a breathy sigh (think of 'gasp')
v	starts with mid pitch and rises (think of 'vaporise')
m	very low and short, with a tiny creak at the end (think of 'mutter')
s	starts quite low and falls even a bit lower (think of 'slide'). It's very hard to distinguish this tone from the mid level tone, but listen for the slight fall, as if the speaker is finishing off a sentence rather than leaving it in mid-air

There is another tone letter, d, which appears very occasionally in words which usually have tone m, for example nam, 'mother'; nad!, 'Hey, Mum!' It's pronounced like v mid rising. For example:

scratch the ground	raub
a hammer	rauj
to be affected/hurt	raug
six	rau
light a fire	rauv
to dip in liquid/wet	raus
kidney	raum

The two 'high' tones – b (high level) and j (high falling) – sometimes influence the pronunciation of the following tones: j, s, and m change to g: v changes to mid level; mid level changes to s. This is especially common in compound nouns, for example nqaij is

MONG

'meat' plus npua; 'pig' is nqaij-npuas, ('pork'), or in combinations involving numbers (eg rau caum, '60' but tsib caug, '50'). However, there are plenty of exceptions to the rule, where tone change doesn't occur when you'd expect it (eg cuaj caum, '90'), and your Mong will be perfectly understandable if you don't make any tone changes. Just be prepared to hear them.

THE LANGUAGE

The two main dialects of Mong spoken in Thailand – Green Mong and White Hmong – are quite similar, except for some aspects of the pronunciation. Many words are exactly the same, a few are just completely different, and many others differ only in the way certain consonants, vowels, or tones are pronounced. The name for 'White Hmong' is an example of the degree of difference in consonants: Green Mong say Moob Dlawb, while White Hmong say Hmoob Dawb. The sentence structure of the two dialects is almost identical. The dialect given here is Green Mong, because it's the one spoken by the majority of Mong living in Thailand.

Forming Sentences

The basic order of words in a Mong sentence is the same as in English: Kuv noj mov, 'I eat rice'. This order of words may be changed if one wishes to present something as a topic, and then say something about it. The word mas often occurs after a topic, at the beginning of a sentence: Mov mas, kuv nyam noj ntau (Rice topic, I like eat a lot), 'As for rice, I like eating (it) a lot'.

Like many other languages spoken in the area, there are no prefixes or suffixes on words, to indicate things like plural for nouns or tense for verbs. Instead, separate words can appear. For example, tau before a verb functions a bit like a past tense marker, or yuav like a future tense marker: Kuv yuav noj mov, 'I will eat rice'. (However, when information like tense is clear from the context, these words need not be added.) Most other words which modify verbs also appear before them; for example tsis, 'not do'; tseem, 'still be doing'; xaav, 'want to do'. Only a few modifying words follow the verb, like the ubiquitous word tau which, when placed after the verb, means 'be able/allowed to do' or 'achieve doing'; and a few come right at the end of the sentence, like taag, 'finish doing'; lawm, 'have done'.

Classifiers

Like other languages in the area, nouns in Mong often occur with a 'classifier' (counting word). A noun without a classifier has no specific reference: dlev, dogs (in general/any old dog). Apart from this, a classifier usually appears: tug dlev (classifier dog), 'the dog'; kuv tug dlev (I classifier dog), 'my dog'; ib tug dle, (one classifier dog), 'a dog/one dog'. Only a few exceptional words, like nam, 'mother' and txiv, 'father', appear without a classifier even in these contexts. Some of the most common classifiers are: tug for humans and animals, and for long, thin things like pens and rivers; lub.

As seen above, the possessor comes before the thing possessed: kuv tug dlev (I classifier dog), 'my dog'. However, adjectives and relative clauses follow the nouns they refer to: dlev luj (dogs big); dlev uas tum (dogs which bite). Nouns which refer to places are generally preceded by a word which tells you where that place is in relation to the speaker: e.g. peg zog, '(an) up-the-hill village'; tim zog, '(an) on-the-other-side village'; ntawm zog; '(a) nearby village'.

Time

Time adverbs generally appear at the beginning of a sentence: Maaj-mam, kuv yuav noj mov, 'After a while, I will eat rice'; intensifying adverbs appear at the end: kuv noj ntau, 'I eat a lot'. Manner adverbs usually appear before the verb they refer to: Kuv maaj-mam noj mov, 'I slowly eat rice'. Many adjectives can also be used to do the job of manner adverbs; these appear after the verb: Kuv noj ceev ceev (I eat fast fast).

Questions

When a question is formed, there's no change in the order of the words as there is in English. For a question with a 'yes' or 'no' answer, the word puas is added directly before the verb: Koj puas

MONG

noj mov? (You question eat rice?). Question words like 'who' or 'what' simply appear in the place of the noun they are referring to: Koj noj dlaab-tsi?, (You eat what?), 'What do you eat?'. If you want to ask how to say something, you can say: Qhov nuav yog dlaab-tsi? (thing this is what?), 'What is this?' or Lus Moob has le-caas (words Mong say how?), 'How do (you) say (it) in Mong?'.

Requests and commands generally include a sentence-final particle: e.g. mas or os to be polite: (Koj) noj mov mas, '(you) eat rice please'; nawb/nawj to be emphatic or encouraging: (Koj) noj mov nawj, ((you) eat rice, OK?), 'Do you eat rice?'.

Question Words

who?	leej-twg
when?	thaum-twg
where?	qhov-twg
which? [classifier -twg]	lub-twg; raab-twg; dlaim-twg
what?	dlaab-tsi
how much (money)?	pis-tsawg (nyaj)
how many?	pis-tsawg

To Be

The verb 'to be' is yog: Nws yog Moob, 'She/He is Mong'. How-ever, this verb doesn't appear nearly as often as its English equiva-lent. Firstly, it isn't needed with adjectives, which are really verbs themselves: Nws zoo heev, 'She/He (is) good very'. Secondly, it isn't used in existential sentences, which use the verb muaj 'have' instead: Puas muaj dlej? (question have water?), 'Is there water/ Do (you) have water?'.

References

There is quite a bit of literature on White Hmong, as spoken in Laos and by most Mong refugees in Western countries, but less for the very similar Green Mong (Mong Njua), spoken by most Mong residents of Thailand. On White Hmong, there's the *White Hmong-English Dictionary* by Ernest Heimbach (South-East Asia Program, Cornell University, NY), and (in French) *Eléments de Grammaire Hmong Blanc* by Jean Mottin, (Don Bosco Press, Bangkok) – the latter often available inexpensively in Thailand.

The only dictionary of Green Mong with an English to Mong section is *English-Mong-English Dictionary* by Lang Xiong, Joua Xiong & Nao Lang Xiong (Pandora Press, Bangkok, reprinted in 1984) also available from DK Book House, Chiang Mai. This is written for Mong speakers, so often English words are explained in Mong rather than translated, but it's still quite useful. *Studies of Green Mong* by TA Lyman include his Grammar of Mong Njua (Green Miao) (Blue Oak Press, Sattley, California, 1979) and his *Dictionary of Mong Njua: a Miao (Meo) Language of South-East Asia* (Mouton, the Hague, 1974).

MONG

WORDS & PHRASES
Greetings & Civilities

Hello.	Nyob zoo.
(lit: live well!)	
How are you?	Koj nyob le caag?
(lit: how are you doing?)	
How are you?	Koj puas noj qaab nyob zoo?
I'm fine.	Kuv noj qaab nyob zoo.

EAT AND LIVE WELL

The phrase Koj puas noj qaab nyob zoo? (How are you?) means 'do you eat and live well?' while the standard reply Kuv noj qaab nyob zoo. (I'm fine.) has a literal meaning of 'I eat and live well.'

MONG

Where are you going?	Koj moog qhov-twg?
I'm going ...	Kuv moog ...
up to the White Mong village	peg zog Moob Dlawb
down to the river valley	nrag haav dlej
to buy vegetables	yuav zaub
home	tsev

Where have you come from?	Koj moog dlaab-tsi lug?
(lit: which place did you go to and come back from?)	
I have come from ...	Kuv moog ... lug.
over at the Yao village	tim zog Cu
I'm just coming to visit you all.	Kuv tuaj saib mej xwb.

Welcome. (lit: you've come!)	Koj tuaj los.
I've arrived.	Kuv tuaj os.
[standard response on entering a village]	

Sit down! (on a chair)	Nyob (ntawm rooj) os.
Have a drink!	Haus dlej.
(lit: drink (some) water!)	
Have you eaten (rice)?	Koj puas tau noj (mov)?
I've finished eating.	Noj taag lawm os.
I haven't eaten yet.	Tseem tsis tau noj

OFF-LIMITS

A household may be declared 'off-limits' to visitors because of illness, etc. It's important to check before you enter.

Are you 'off-limits'?	Mej puas caiv os?
We are not 'off-limits'.	Peb tsis caiv os.

YOU MAY HEAR ...

Come in! (lit: ... into the house)   Lug tsev mas.

You don't have to take off your shoes before entering a
house, but it's polite to take off your hat.

Thank you (very much).	Ua tsaug (ntau ntau).
You're welcome.	Tsis ua le caag.
I'll be going back (home).	Kuv yuav rov qaab moog (tsev).
(Go, and) come again!	Moog ho tuaj nawb!
Goodbye.	Sib ntsib dlua.
(lit: we'll meet again.)	

Small Talk

What is your name?	Koj lub npe hu le caag?
My name is ...	Kuv lub npe hu ua ...
Where do you live?	Koj nyob qhov-twg?
I live in [name of country].	Kuv nyob huv ...
Have you got ...?	Koj puas muaj ...?
a wife	tug quas-puj
a husband	tug quas-yawg
brothers and sisters	kwv-tij viv-ncaug
mother and father	nam hab txiv
(ie are they alive?)	
children	miv-nyuas

MONG

WHICH LANGUAGE?

I don't understand.	Kuv tsis to-taub.
Do you speak ...?	Koj has lug ... puas tau?
English [language]	Aas-kiv
Thai [language]	Thaib
Chinese [language]	Suav
Burmese [language]	Maab
French [language]	Faab-kis

How many brothers and sisters do you have?	Koj nam yug tau mej pis-tsawg leej?
(lit: how many of you all did your mother gave birth to?)	
How many children have you?	Koj muaj pis-tsawg tug miv-nyuas?
I have only one (person).	Kuv muaj ib leeg xwb.
I have four (people).	Kuv muaj plaub leeg.

Accommodation & Meals

May I sleep in your house?	Kuv thov su huv koj tsev puas tau?
If I stay one night, how much is it?	Yog kuv pw ib mo, pis-tsawg nyaj?

MONG

| One night is 20 baht. | Ib mo yog neeg-nkaum Nbaj nyaj. |
| Where shall I put my things? | Kuv tso kuv cov khoom rua qhov-twg? |

Do you have a (lit: one) ...?	Koj puas muaj ib ...?
blanket	dlaim choj
flashlight (torch)	lub teeb nyem
lamp	lub teeb
mattress	dlaim tswm-zooj
mosquito net	lub vij-tsam (kauv yoov)
pillow	lub hauv-ncoo
woven mat	dlaim lev

I would like to buy ...	Kuv xaav yuav ...
(flashlight) batteries	roj teeb
a chicken	ib tug qab
eggs	qai
fish	ntseg
meat	nqaj
pork	nqaj-npuas
soap	xa-buj

How much is ...?	... yog pis-tsawg nyaj?
one animal	ib tug ...
one kg	ib kis-lus ...

| Are you willing to make ... for me to eat? | Koj puas kaam ua ... rau kuv noj? |
| beans | taum |

BROTHERS, SISTERS ... COUSINS

In Mong, the term kwv-tij viv-ncaug ('brothers and sisters') includes patrilineal cousins.

MONG

AT THE TABLE

Eat up, everybody!	Sawv-dlawg noj!
Drink whisky!	Haus cawv!
I can't eat chillies.	Kuv noj hov-txob tsis tau.
Have you got salt?	Koj puas muaj ntsev.
It's very tasty.	Qaab qaab kawg.

beef	nqaj-nyug
buffalo meat	nqaj-twm
chicken	nqaj-qab
corn	pob-kws
eggplant	lws-ntev
jackfruit	txiv-plaab-nyug
pork	nqaj-npuas
pumpkin	taub-dlaag
(cooked) rice	mov
taro	qos-tsw-haa
vegetables	zaub

I would like to eat ...	Kuv xaav noj ...
banana	txiv-tsawb
fruit	txiv
mango	txiv-txhais

I would like to get ...	Kuv xaav tau ...
a (small) bowl	ib lub ntim
a pair of chopsticks	ib txwg rawg
a (tea) cup	ib lub khob
hot water	dlej kub
a knife	ib raab rag
a spoon	ib raab dlav

Do you smoke tobacco?	Koj puas haus luam-yeeb?
I don't smoke tobacco.	Kuv tsis haus luam-yeeb.
I don't smoke opium.	Kuv tsis haus yeeb.

Are you sleepy?	Koj puas tsaug-zug?
I'm very sleepy.	Kuv tsaug tsaug-zug le.
I'm very tired/lethargic.	Kuv nkeeg nkeeg le.

Traditional Life & Crafts

MONG

spirit/demon	dlaab
tame household spirit	dlaab nyeg
wild jungle spirit	dlaab qus
friendly spirits	neeb
[who help the shaman to cure illness, etc]	
shaman/traditional doctor	tug txiv neeb
perform the spirit rites	ua neeb
spirit altar	thaaj neeb
[shelf in the home for articles of spirit worship]	
weaving loom	(lub) ntus
bamboo pipes	(raab) qeej
drum/gong	(lub) nruag
flute	(lub) raaj nplaim
(small) bamboo flute	(lub) raaj pum-liv
three finger flute	(lub) raaj nploog

HAPPY NEW YEAR!

If you happen to be among Mong speakers over the New Year, here are some useful terms to know.

New Year	peb caug
celebrate the New Year	noj peb caug
(lit: eat the 30th)	
rice cakes	ncuav
[special for New Year, made of pounded sticky rice]	
celebrate the first new rice of the season	noj mov nplej tshab
(lit: eat new rice)	

MONG

DID YOU KNOW ...	A jew's-harp, (raab) ncaas, is usually used only in courting. Mong courtship is carried out under a veil of secrecy. The young man might go to the girl's house at night, and beckon her through her bedroom wall with the ncaas. Any public show of physical affection, even between married couples, is found embarrassing.

full moon	hli nraa
waning moon	hli nqeg
waning half moon	hli phua qaab thoob
(lit: split the base of the bucket moon)	
new moon (lit: waxing one)	xab ib
waxing moon	hli xab
eclipse of the moon	dlaab noj hli
(lit: spirits eat moon)	
Christian Church	lub tsev pe Vaaj-tswv
(lit: house to bow down before God)	
place of worship	lub tsev teev ntuj
(lit: house to call on the heavens)	
King of the heavens	Huab Tais Ntuj
[legendary God-like figure]	
the legendary Mong creator	Saub
Christian God	Vaaj Tswv Saub
(lit: King Lord Creator)	
to marry [for women]	yuav quas-yawg
(lit: obtain a husband)	
to marry [for men]	yuav quas-puj
(lit: obtain a wife)	

MONG

Shopping

Do you want to buy a ...?	Koj puas xaav yuav ib ...?

I want to buy a ...	Kuv xaav yuav ib ...
(round) bangle [brass or copper]	lub kauj toog-npaab
bracelet [usually gold or silver]	txuj saug teg
earring	lub kauj-ntseg
hat	lub kaus-mom
leather belt	txuj hlaab tawv
pair of earrings [more elaborate]	txwg qhws-ntsej
pair of leggings/puttees	nkawm nrhoob
(pair of) pants	lub rig
piece of embroidery/ appliqué/cross-stitch work (lit: flower cloth)	dlaim paaj-ntaub
ring	nti nplhaib
shirt/jacket	lub tsho
shoulder bag	lub naab thoob-puab
silver neck ring	lub paug
skirt	dlaim tab

How much will you give me?	Koj yuav muab pis-tsawg nyaj rau kuv?

white	dlawb
black	dlub
red	lab
yellow	dlaaj
dark blue/green	ntsuab
blue, purple	xav

Health

wash (one's) hands/body	ntxuav tes/cev
go to the toilet [polite]	moog plob
urinate	tso zig
defecate	tso quav

MONG

Is Everybody Happy?

In Mong, questions about whether you're happy or sad relate - in literal terms - to the health of your liver.

to be happy	zoo sab
	(lit: be good (in the) liver)
to be sad	tsis zoo sab
	(lit: not be good (in the) liver)
	chim sab
	(lit: be angry/sad (in the) liver)

My ... hurts.	Kuv mob ...
ear	pob-ntseg
eye(s)	qhov-muag
head	taub-hau
heart	plawv
leg/foot	taw
lower back	dluav
stomach	plaab
tooth	nav

My arm is broken.	Kuv txhais teg luv.
I have malaria.	Kuv mob npaws.
I have diarrhoea.	Kuv thoj plaab.
I am constipated.	Kuv mob plaab cem-quav.
Would you carry me?	Koj puas kaam aub kuv?

Is there ... here?	Ntawm nuav puas muaj ...?
medicine	tshuaj
a doctor	ib tug kws tshuaj

Directions & the Countryside

Which is the path to ...?	Txuj kev uas moog rau ...
	yog txuj kev twg?
the Yao village	lub zog Cu
the bus	lub tsheb npa

Is the path good?	Txuj kev puas zoo?
Not so good.	Tsis zoo.
Go straight ahead.	Ncaaj nraim moog.
Can (one) ride a motorcycle here?	Caij lub mos-tos moog ntawd puas tau?
Would you take me there by motorcycle?	Koj puas kaam caij lub mos-tos coj kuv?
Would you come with me?	Koj puas kaam nrug kuv moog ntawd?
Would you carry my things?	Koj puas kaam aub kuv cov khoom?
How much (money) would you like?	Koj yuav pis-tsawg nyaj?

MONG

path/road	(txuj) kev
bridge	(tug) choj
cliff	(lub) pob-tsua
[unirrigated] field	(dlaim) teb
[irrigated – paddy] field	(dlaim) laj
fire	hluav-tawg
moon	(lub) hli
mountain	(lub) roob
river/stream	(tug) dlej
smoke	paa-tawg
stone	(lub) pob-zeb
sun	(lub) nub
tree	(tug) ntoo
valley	(lub) haav

to go	moog
to come	tuaj
to come/return home	lug
to ascend	nce
to descend	nqeeg

MONG

side/direction	saab
right side	saab xis
left side	saab laug
above/top	saum
underneath	huv qaab
inside	huv
in front	tom ntej
behind	tom qaab
up the slope	peg
down the slope	nrag
across/on the other side	tim
over there	tom
nearby	ntawm

Weather

The sun is shining.	Lub nub ci.
It's raining.	(Ntuj) lug naag.
(lit: (sky) flows rain)	
It's hailing.	Ntuj lug lawg.
It's cloudy.	Tsaus huab.
It's foggy.	Huab ntsau-tsawv.
The path is slippery.	Txuj kev nplua nplua.
It's cold [weather].	No no le.
It's warm.	Suv suv le.
(It's) wet.	Ntub.

Ethnic Groups

[village: lub zog ...; person: ib tug ...]

Lahu	Lub-hej; Luab
Akha	Khuaj; Phub-thawj
Lisu	Lij-xub
Mong (Meo)	Moob
Mien (Yao)	Cu
Shan	(Meg) Ncuav; Nyawj
Northern Thai	(Meg) Ncuav; Kuj-loom
Thai	Thaib

Chinese	Suav
Karen	Yaas
Indian	Khej
Westerner, European	Huab-lab

MONG

People
(Classifier: tug)

person	tuab-neeg
friend	phooj-ywg
man	txiv-neej
woman	quas-puj
young unmarried man	hluas-nraug
young unmarried woman	hluas-nkauj
old man	yawg laug
old woman	puj
headman	thawj-coj
baby	miv-nyuas mog-lab

MONG

Animals

barking deer [small deer]	kauv
bear	dlais
[large] bee	ntaab
[small] bee	muv
bird	noog
body lice	tuv
cat	miv
cockroach	laum
cow	nyuj
dog	dlev

SOME USEFUL WORDS

to remember	ncu qaab
to forget	nov qaab
to sell	muag
to buy	yuav
to give	pub
to take/pick up	muab
to have a chat	sib thaam
to sing	hu nkauj
to meet	ntsib
quickly	ceev ceev
slowly	maaj-mam
silver	nyaj-dlawb
gold	kub
country	teb-chaws
market	kab-khw
town/city	nroog
this	qhov nuav
that	qhov ntawd
(very) beautiful	zoo-nkauj (taag taag)
bad, ugly	phem

elephant	ntxhw
a fly	yoov
gibbon	cuam
head lice	ntshauv
horse	neeg
house rat	tsuag
jungle fowl	yij
leech	nplaj-hab
monkey	lab
mule	luj-txwv
(long-quilled) porcupine	tsaug
sambar deer [large deer]	muas-lwj
snake	naab
squirrel	naag-ncuav
tiger	tsuv
water buffalo	twm
wild boar	npua-teb

MONG

Numbers & Classifiers

1	ib	7	xyaa
2	ob	8	yim
3	peb	9	cuaj
4	plaub	10	kaum
5	tsib	11	kaum ib
6	rau	12	kaum ob

Twenty is neeg-nkaum. Round numbers from 30 to 90, are made with the number plus caum (caug after tone -b, but not after -j).

30	peb caug (lit: 3, 10)	90	cuaj caum (lit: 9, 10)

MONG

The hundreds are made with the number plus 100, pua (puas after tones -b or -j); thousands are the number plus 1000, phaav.

100	ib puas	700	xyaa pua
2000	ob phaav phaav	40,000	plaub caug

Combinations go from largest to smallest:

1991	ib phaav cuaj puas cuaj caum ib
555	tsib puas tsib caug tsib
35	peb caug tsib

Time Words

Some basic time words can be used as classifiers themselves:

day	nub
10 days	kaum nub
night	mos
month	hlis
four months	plaub hlis
year	xyoo
six years	rau xyoo

yesterday	naag-mo
today	nub nuav
tomorrow	pig-kis
day after tomorrow	quas-nraus
this morning	nub nuav sawv-ntxuv
this evening	nub nuav tsaus-ntuj

CULTURE

The Mien are an ethnic group known to the Thai, the Lao and the Chinese as Yao, and to the Vietnamese as Dao (pronounced *Zao*). Under the name of Yao they have figured for centuries in Chinese official records, and in modern times, in Western anthropological and travel literature. Mien means 'people', and in a narrower sense it means 'Mien people' as opposed to everybody else. To specify the narrower sense of 'Mien people' they add Iu in front, yielding a full name Iu Mien. Iu is pronounced 'EE-oo'.

The Mien language is fairly closely related to the language of the Mong. Mien culture has been much influenced by Chinese culture. Perhaps 50% of the ordinary vocabulary of the Mien language is of Chinese origin, and the proportion of Chinese words in the Mien ritual language may be 90%. The pronunciation of the Chinese words suggests that they were borrowed from Old Cantonese. However the Mien claim that they cannot understand modern Cantonese, though they can speak south-western Mandarin, the lingua franca of the Golden Triangle area.

Along with Old Cantonese words, the Mien borrowed their associated Chinese written characters. Thus the Mien acquired a system of writing which they have had now for several centuries, and use to record their rituals, keep family records, and write contracts and letters. This long-standing tradition of writing makes the Mien unique among the hill tribes in Thailand. Traditionally Mien boys are taught to read and write by their fathers or by Chinese teachers hired by the village. These days Mien elders are worried because fewer boys are learning the Chinese characters and this writing is integral to the Mien religion.

Apart from the Chinese script there are Thai-based and Roman-based systems for writing Mien which have been devised for the Mien by Western missionaries. It's one of these Roman scripts, as further developed by the Mien, that is used in this phrasebook. This script is widely used by the Mien in China and to a lesser degree by Mien refugees in the West.

Mien (Yao) in Thailand

MIEN

The Mien have a story of descent from P'an Hu, a pet dog in the palace of a Chinese emperor, which links them with the most ancient period of Chinese history. Although their early history is uncertain, they have a tradition of having crossed the sea in what must have been the 14th century. They also have a document which has been called the 'Yao Charter' or the 'Mien passport'. This is a Chinese imperial edict which exempts the descendants of P'an Hu, now titled 'P'an Wang' (King P'an), from all taxes and levies, and allows them freedom to cultivate all the mountains of the empire. The Mien originated in China, where most of them still live, and migrated down into northern Vietnam, Laos and Thailand in relatively recent times.

The total population of Mien speakers is about 2 million, including about 45,000 in Thailand and some 1.4 million in China. Most of the rest are in northern Vietnam (520,000), with substantial numbers in northern Laos (15,000) and some refugees from Laos in Western countries. The Yao nationality in China also includes speakers of closely related dialects and of two other languages, Bunu and Lajia, which have a total population of about a million more. The Mien in Thailand are concentrated in the extreme north, mainly Chiang Rai, Phayao and Nan provinces, with a few villages scattered further south. Some of the most easily accessible villages north-west of Chiang Rai are Mien; you may pass a Mien village on the way to a Lahu, Akha or Lisu village at a higher altitude, as the Mien often attempt to get some valley land which can be irrigated.

Mien villages are described as having 'no village gate, ceremonial building or dancing ground – sometimes not even a well-defined village area'. You'll know that a village is Mien if you come across 'groups of black-turbaned, red-ruffed women on low stools bending over their embroidery' (*Peoples of the Golden Triangle*, Lewis & Lewis). For a village site, Mien favour gradual slopes, with steeper slopes above and below. Mien villages vary in size; the norm is 10 to 25 houses, but some villages may have more than 200 houses.

MIEN

These houses are built directly on the ground, with walls of wood or bamboo; they're often much larger than those of other hill tribes. The roof is commonly made of thatched grass, but sometimes wooden shingles, large leaves or even sheets of roofing metal are used. There are three doors to the outside. At one end the men's door leads into the area where guests are received; at the other end is the women's door leading to the kitchen, and in the front of the house is the Big Door, so called because of its importance in special ceremonies. Right opposite the Big Door inside the house is the ancestral altar. There are two main stoves: one where the family's food is cooked, and one where the pigs' food is cooked. It's believed that a spirit dwells in the stoves, so you mustn't put your feet on them or sit with your back against them.

The household normally consists of an extended family. This comprises a husband and wife, one or more married sons and their families, and the unmarried children. When a woman marries she joins her husband's household. Households can be quite large; 20 people isn't unusual, and households of up to 60 are not unknown.

The Mien religion represents a fusion of animism, ancestor worship and Taosim. The Mien believe in a great number of spirits, ranging from house spirits to nature spirits, the latter being the proprietors of such things as streams, trees and regions. It is necessary to maintain good relations with both the spirits and the ancestors. If propitiated, the ancestors will protect everyone in the household, but if either spirits or ancestors become displeased they can bring trouble, such as sickness or accidents.

The Taosim that the Mien follow was borrowed from the Chinese in the 13th and 14th centuries, and differs from contemporary Chinese Taoism. The Mien believe in a hierarchy of celestial functionaries. They have rites of different grades for ordaining postulants, introducing postulants to the Taoist pantheon, guaranteeing them entry into the realm of the ancestors when they die, and so on.

Every Mien woman is an expert at embroidery. Her pièce de résistance is her embroidered trousers. Mien women also produce ornate caps for their young children and embellish shoulder bags with embroidery, usually with a variety of traditional stitches. On festive occasions women and children wear silver neck-rings. Women also wear a variety of silver finger rings as well as silver bracelets. The Mien have highly skilled silversmiths, who turn out beautiful silver butterflies, birds, fish and flowers, often with cloisonné. They also have religious paintings, depicting deities and functionaries of the afterworld – a popular art tradition which stems from Chinese Taoist religious art. These paintings are products of the Mien's centuries-old adherence to Taoism of the Southern School, of which the Mien seem to be the only modern representatives. They treat these paintings with the greatest respect, for they are literally the abode, or rather the raiment, of the gods.

MIEN

But Western art collectors put a high value on them, and some Mien families, in dire straits because of the Indochina War or other conditions of modern life, have been forced to sell them.

For further readings on Mien culture in general you may consult Paul & Elaine Lewis's superbly illustrated book *Peoples of the Golden Triangle*. To read more about the Mien religious paintings and the practices and beliefs that go with them, see *Yao Ceremonial Paintings* by Jacques Lemoine (White Lotus, Bangkok, 1982); this book too has many beautiful colour pictures, and is widely available in Thailand.

SOUNDS
Vowels

MIEN

i	as the English 'ee' in 'see'
e	as the English 'e' in 'set'
ae	as the English 'a' in 'apple'
aa	as the American 'o' in 'odd' or British 'ah' in 'Shah'
a	a short version of aa or as the American 'awe' or British 'o' in 'odd'
o	as the American 'owe' or British 'awe' but with the lips rounded narrowly
u	as the 'u' but with the lips narrowly rounded
ei	as the 'ay' in 'say'
ai	as the 'y' in 'my' said quickly
aai	as the 'y' in 'my' said slowly
oi	as the 'oy' in 'boy'
iu	like ee-oo said smoothly and quickly in one syllable
eu	like ay-oo said smoothly and quickly in one syllable
au	like 'how' said quickly
aau	like 'how' said slowly
ou	as the 'ur' sound of British 'burr' (the 'r' is not pronounced) followed smoothly and quickly by a strongly rounded 'oo': 'ur-oo'
ie	as the American 'ia' in 'via', or British 'ear' (the 'r' is not pronounced)

_{.10} as the 'our' in British 'tour' (the 'r' is not pronounced), with strong lip-rounding for the 'u' part; as the American 'ui' in 'fluid' or 'druid'

Consonants

Mien, like the other languages discussed here, has aspirated and unaspirated sounds. For information on how to pronounce them, see the Introduction, page 15.

At the beginning of the syllable Mien p, t and k represent the aspirated sounds; c is an aspirated 'ts' sound as in English borrowed words such as 'tsetse' or 'tsunami', and q is like an aspirated 'ch' as in English 'chew'.

At the beginning of the syllable Mien b, d and g are the unaspirated sounds of 'p', 't' and 'k' as in 'spill', 'still' and 'skill'; z is the unaspirated 'ts' as in English 'hats off', pronounced smoothly together, and j is like the unaspirated 'ch' as in English 'catch up'.

The voiced sounds like English 'b', 'd' and 'g' are written with mb, nd and nq. These are pronounced very distinctly (fully voiced); note especially that nq represents 'g'. Similarly, nz represents 'dz' ('d' plus 'z') and nj represents a 'j'-like sound as in 'judge'.

Ng is like the 'ng' sounds of English 'singing', but may also come at the beginning of a syllable. Ny represents a single sound like English 'ni' in 'onion' or 'union'.

Mien has four sounds preceded by a breath exhaled through the nose (preaspirated nasals); these are hm, hn, hny and hng.

Hl is like English 'h' mixed with and followed by 'l'. Hi followed by a vowel is like the beginning of English 'Hugh', that is, like 'h' plus 'y'. Hu followed by a vowel is like English 'wh' in 'where' as contrasted with 'w' as in 'wear', that is, like 'h' plus 'w'.

When p, t, k come at the end of a syllable they're not exploded (that is, they're not only not aspirated, but also not even released). Q at the end of a syllable represents a catch in the throat (glottal stop), as in the middle of English 'oh-oh'.

Note that any one of h, v, z, x, and c at the end of a syllable represents the tone of that syllable, not a consonant; see the following section on tones.

Tones

Every syllable in Mien has a fixed pitch or melody known as its tone. A syllable must be said with the right tone before it can be recognised as having a meaning. Tones are indicated in the spelling system by a silent consonant at the end of the syllable: either h, v, z, x or c, and a sixth tone indicated by the absence of any of these five consonants. For example, maaih means 'to have'; maaiz means 'to buy'; maaic means 'to sell'. These tones have the following sounds:

unmarked	medium-high level
-v	high rising-falling
-h	mid falling
-x	medium-low rising
-z	low rising-falling
-c	low level

MIEN

THE LANGUAGE

Unlike some other hill tribe languages of Thailand and Laos, Iu Mien is not very broken up dialectically. Thus the Mien of Thailand speak a dialect virtually identical with the Mien of Laos, and very close to the dialect of most of the same ethnic group in China and Vietnam.

Forming Sentences

The order of the sentence in Mien is the same as English, that is subject-verb-object. For example, Yie nyanc hnaangx goes word for word into English, 'I eat rice'. The negative comes immediately in front of the verb; thus Yie mingh, 'I go', negates as Yie maiv mingh, or in contracted form Yie mv mingh, 'I don't go', literally 'I not go'. When making a request or command, to be polite you should add the particle at the end of the sentence, for example Bieqc biauv oc (lit: enter house. oh!) which is to say 'Please come in'.

The standard response to questions is to repeat the verb:

| Do you smoke tobacco? | Meih buov inh-mbiaatc nyaae? |
| Yes, I do (smoke). | Buov. |

Pronouns

I/me	yie
you (singular)	meih
he/she/it, him/her	ninh

These pronouns are made plural by adding mbuo:

we/us	yie mbuo
you (plural)	meih mbuo
they/them	ninh mbuo or na-mbuo

To make the possessive form one adds nyei to the singular or plural form of the pronoun, for example meih nyei, 'your' (belonging to you, singular); meih mbuo nyei, 'your' (belonging to you, plural). Yie nyei, 'my' has an alternative form; mv nyei.

Question Words

who?	haiv dauh
what?	haiv nyungc
when?	haiv zanc
where?	haiv nda
how much?	buqc-ziax
how many? [+ classifier]	buqc-ziax ...
which? [+ classifier + noun]	haiv ...?
for what purpose/in order to do what?	zouc haiv nyung

MIEN

To Be

Mien has several verbs 'to be', but they are not as frequent as in some languages because they are not used with adjectives, which are verbs in their own right, nor with existentials, which instead use the verb maaih, 'to have, there is/are', as in:

The rice (is) very good.	Hnaangx khuv haic.
Is there water/Do you have water?	Uom maaih nyae?

References

Mien is fairly well served by the *Yao-English Dictionary* by Sylvia Lombard (Cornell University South-East Asia Program Data Paper series, 1968), but the only grammar available is an unpublished University of California Berkley PhD thesis by Christopher Court; this may eventually be more widely available.

WORDS & PHRASES
Greetings & Civilities

How are you? (lit: are you well?)	Meih yiem longx nyae?
Fine.	Longx nyae.
Where are you going?	Meih mingh haiv hdau?
I'm returning home.	Yie nzuonx uov biauv.
I'm going to ...	Yie mingh ...
the Mien village	Mienh nyei laangz
wash myself	nzaaaux sin
the Akha village	Janh-aa-khaa nyei laangz
Where have you come from?	Mei yiem haix daaih?
I've come for a visit.	Yie daaih nziaauc.
I've come from the Northern Thai village.	Yie yiem Janh-kor-lorkv nyei laangz daaih.

Have you eaten (rice)?	Meih mv gaengh nyanc hnaangx saa?
(I) have eaten already.	Nyanc liuz aq.
(I) have not eaten yet.	Mv kaengh nyanc oc.
Come inside the house!	Bieqc biauv oc!
Drink (some) tea!	Hopv kaax zaah!
Drink (some) water!	Hopv uom oc!
Thank you.	Laengz zingh.
Very good.	Longx haic ni aa.
You're welcome.	Mv penx haiv nyungc lorq.
(lit: it's nothing)	
Goodbye. (lit: go visit us)	Mingh nziaauc oc!
[said by person who is leaving]	
Goodbye.	Mingh longz oc.
[said by person who is staying]	
Please come again!	Dih hnoi aengz daaih nziaauc oc!

MIEN

Small Talk

Where do you live?	Meih yiem haiv ndau?
I live in ...	Yie yiem ...
the USA	A-mev-riv-kaa deih-bung
Australia	Australia deih-bung

WHICH LANGUAGE?

I don't understand.	Yie mv bieqc hnyiouv.
Do you know the ... language?	Mieh hiuv duqv ... waac nyae?
English	angkitv
Thai	anh-taiv
Chinese	anh-kaeqv
Burmese	anh-pamaah

MIEN

What is your name?	Meih heuc haiv nyungc?
My name is ...	Yie heuc ...
Have you got ...?	Meih maaih ...?
a wife	auv mic aq
a husband	nqox mic aq
brothers and sisters	muah-doic nyae
Are your parents still alive?	Meih nyei domh-mienh corc yiem nyae?
How many brothers and sisters have you got?	Meih maaih mbuqc-ziex muaz?
How many children have you got?	Meih maaih mbuqc ziexdauh fuqc-jueiv?

Accommodation & Meals

May I sleep in your house?	Yie tov bueix meih nyei biauv duqv nyae?
If I stay one night, how much is it?	Se gorngv yie yiem yietc muonz norq, mbuqcziexorqv?
One night is 20 baht.	Yietc muonz nyic-ziepc mbaatv.
Where shall I put my things down?	Yie nyei gaqc-naiv an haiv ndau?
How much is ...?	... mbuqc-ziex orqv?
one	Yietc norm
one chicken	Yietc norm jae
one kg	Yietc kilo

SOME USEFUL WORDS

to sell	maaic
to buy	maaiz
to give	bun
to take/bring	dorh
to sing	baux nzung
to meet	buangh
to be sad	nzaaug
to remember	njangz
to forget	laqc-kuqv
to marry	dorng jaa
to have a conversation	gorngv waac
quickly	siepv
slowly	donc
place/district/country	deic-bung
market	hei
town	mungv
silver/money	nyaanh
gold	jiem
this	naiv
that	naic
that (over there)	uov

MIEN

Will you cook me some ...?	Tov meih zouv deix ... bun yie oc?
(cooked) rice	hnaangx
pork	dungh-orv
chicken	jaeh-orv
vegetables	laih-maeng
pumpkin	fuqc-nyomv
eggplant	jiah
beans	dopc
eggs	jaux

AT THE TABLE

Please eat until you're full!	Nyanc beuv hnaangx oc!
Drink whisky!	Hopv diuv oc!
I can't eat chillies.	Yie nyanc maiv duqv fanh-ziu.
Have you got salt?	Meih maaih nzaauv nyae?
It's very delicious.	Naic kuv haic ni aa!

Do you have (a) ...?   Meih maaih ... nyae?
   blanket   suanqx
   flashlight (torch)   dienx tongh
   lamp   dang
   mat   ziqc
   mattress   suangh-timh-hoz
   mosquito net   mungh-dangx
   pillow   nzuom-dauh

Can I buy ...?   Yie maaiz ... duqv nyae?
   a chicken   jae
   eggs   jaux
   fish   biaux
   (flashlight) batteries   dienx tongh ndie
   meat   orv
   pork   tungh-orv
   soap   sabu

Can you give me ...?   Tov meih bun ... yie duqv nyae?
   some fruit   deix biouv
   some bananas   deix normh-ziuh-biouv
   some mangoes   deix mamong biouv
   a bowl   norm nzormc
   a pair of chopsticks   sung zouc
   a spoon   norm ken
   a (small) knife   zung nzuqc-dorn
   some hot water   diex uomh-jorm

MIEN

Do you smoke tobacco?	Meih buov inh-mbiaatc nyae?
I don't smoke opium.	Yie mv buov in.
Are you sleepy?	Meih mh zing nyuix nyae?
I am very sleepy.	Yie mh zing nyuix haic.
I am very tired.	Yie kov taic.

Traditional Life & Crafts

Christian church	la paaix dorngh
house-altar	mienh-paih
New Year	siangh-hnyaangx
[celebrated at Chinese New Year]	
celebrate the New Year	jie siangh-hnyaangh
moon	hlaax
eclipse of the moon	tinh gauv nyac hlaax

MIEN

highest god [non-Christian]	Nyutc-taix hungh
God [Christian; heavenly king]	Tinh-hungh
spirit [non-Christian]	mienv
shaman [spirit-appeasing person]	sipc-mienv mienh
pastor [Christian]	finh-saeng diex

drum	nzoc
gong [with centre bump]	mang
gong [without centre bump]	lorz

> **DID YOU KNOW ...** Tinh gauv nyac hlaax ('eclipse of the moon') literally means 'heavenly dog eats the moon'.

MIEN

Shopping

| How much is it? | Meih bun duqv mbuqc-ziex? |
| Do you want to buy a ...? | Meih oix maaiz ... nyae? |

I want to buy a ...	Yie oix maaiz ...
belt	houh-hlaang
bracelet	norm jiemh
[large silver] button	laqc-kauh-beih
pants	houx
purse	kapaux
shirt	lui
shoulder bag	mbuoqc-jorngx
silver necklace	jaangh-waanh

white	baeqc
black	jieqv
red	siqv
yellow	yangh
blue	mbouv
green	maeng
beautiful	nzueic

Health

to wash one's hands	nzaaux buoz
to wash one's body	nzaaux sin

go to defecate   mingh pungx nqaiv
[not euphemistic, but not as strong as in English]
go to urinate   mingh pungh yiez

My ... hurts.	Yie nyei ... mun.
arm/hand	buoz
chest	aqv-kuotv
ear	mh-normh
eye(s)	mh zing
head	mh nqorngv
leg/foot	zaux
lower back	jaaiv
stomach	gaih sia
tooth	nyaah

My arm is broken.	Mv nyei buoz nauv mic aq.
I have diarrhoea.	Mv nyei gaiz-sia fiex.
I am constipated.	Yie bungz nqaiv baangz.

Have you got medicine?	Meih maaih ndie nyae?
Is there a doctor here?	Naiv ndau maaih naih-morx
[Western-style]	nyae?
Can you carry me there?	Meih nyiax dorh yie mingh
	duqv nyae?

MIEN

GO TO THE FOREST

The verb mingh lomc ('to go to the bathroom') has
a literal meaning of 'to go to the forest'.

Directions & the Countryside

Where is the path to ...?	Haiv diuh jauv mingh ...?
the Mien village	(Iuh-) Mienh nyei laangz
the bus	lotv me zaamc

Is that path good?	Naic diuh jauv longx nyae?
Not so good.	Mv dongc haix longx.
Go straight ahead.	Mingh zaqc.

Can a motorcycle go there?   Lotv kueangh haih yangh
     naic diuh jauv mingh nyae?

Can you take me there   Meih dorh lotv kueangh tor
   by motorcycle?   yie mingh naic duqv nyae?

Can you accompany me?   Meih bienz yie mingh duqv
     nyae?

Can you carry my things?   Meih tengh yie dorh yie
     nyei gaqc-naiv mingh
     duqv nyae?

How much money should I   Yie aa-zuqc bun nyaanh
   give you?   meih mbuqc-ziex orq?

bridge	jiouh
cliff	mbaengx
[unirrigated, sloping] field	ndeic
[irrigated, flat] field	lingh
fire	douz
moon	hlaax
mountain	mbong
river	ndaih
rock	laqc-bieiv
smoke	douh-sioux
stream/brook	ndoqv
sun	mbaqc-hnoi
tree	ndiangx
valley	mbai

MIEN

side	maengh or jieqv
path/way/method/direction	jauv
right side	mbiauuc maengx
left side	zaaix maengx
above	guh nguaaic
below	gaih ndieqv
in front	nzaqc hmien
behind	nqaqc haav maengx
to go (away from where speaker is now)	mingh
to come (towards where speaker is now)	daaih
to go up	faux
to go down	njiec

MIEN

Weather

The sun is shining.	Nyutc ziux jienv.
It's raining.	Duih mbiungc.
It's hailing.	Duih mborqc.
The sky is overcast and cloudy.	Lungh opv.
The path is slippery.	Jauv mbiaangc.
The path is wet.	Jauv ndorn.
I'm cold.	Yie juangv.
I'm hot.	Yie yuoqv.
I'm wet.	Yie ndorn.

Ethnic Groups

The terms for most non-Mien ethnic groups are prefaced with the word janh, uncombined janx, 'foreigner, non-Mien person'.

Mien, Iu Mien (Yao)	Mienh or Iuh Mienh
White Hmong person	Janh-baeqc-miuh
Lahu person	Janh-lor-hec
Akha person	Janh-aav-kaah
Lisu person	Janh-lih-sorv
Northern Thai person	Janh-gor-lorkv
Thai person	Janh-taiv
Chinese person	Janh-kaeqv
European (lit: white foreigner)	Janh-baeqc

He is an American.   Ninh Janh-a-mev-riv-kaa.

People

person	mienh
friend	aah-nziaauc doic
man	mh-jaangc dorn
woman	mh-sieqv dorn
young unmarried man	houh-saeng
old man	ongh-gox
old woman	gux
headman	daauh-mien or mienh-gox
baby	guh-nguaaz

Animals

barking deer	jung
bear	jiepv
bee	mueiz
bird	norqv
cat	lomh-miu
cattle	ngongh
dog	juv
elephant	zaangz

MIEN

a fly	mungz
horse	maaz
jungle fowl	norqv jae
leech	biom
monkey	mbing
mule	lorh
rat	nauz
sambar deer	njaeh
snake	naang
squirrel	mbopv
tiger	ndah-mauh
water buffalo	su-ngongh
wild boar	hieh-dungz

MIEN

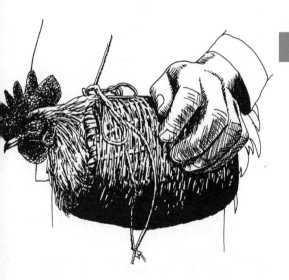

Numbers & Classifiers

Counting in Mien requires a classifier (a counting help-word) after the number. The number plus the classifier come before the noun being counted, so that, for instance, i duih jauv, 'two paths', is literally 'two-long-thing-path'. The noun itself does not change to mark the plural. The common classifier is norm but this cannot be used with humans and higher-order animals, which take dauh (which originally meant 'head'). For example, buo dauh mienh, 'three persons', literally means 'three higher-order-being person'. As for the numbers, the simple numbers one to nine are expressed by native Mien words, while with tens and hundreds Chinese-derived numerals are used, as shown below.

MIEN

1	yietc	11	ziepc-yietv
2	i	12	ziepc-nyeic
3	buo	13	ziepc-faam
4	biei	14	ziepc-feix
5	biaa	15	ziepc-hmmz
6	juqv	16	ziepc-luoqc
7	siec	17	ziepc-cietv
8	hietc	18	ziepc-betv
9	nduoh	19	ziepc-juov
10	ziepc	20	nyic-ziepc

21	nyic-ziepc-yietv	92	juov-ziepc-nyeic
22	nyic-ziepc-nyeic	93	juov-ziepc-faam
23	nyic-ziepc-faam	200	nyei-baeqv
90	juov-ziepc	500	hmmz-baeqv
91	juov-ziepc-yietv		

Hmm sounds like English 'Hmm', the English cry of doubt or wondering.

Numbers higher than 99 are formed by using the number (one to 10) plus the word for thousand, cin; ten thousand, waanc

(Chinese) or muenx (Thai); a hundred thousand, sinx, or a million, laanh:

4000	biei-cin	10,000	yietc-waanc
600,000	juqv sin	8 million	hietc-laanh

Combinations go from largest to smallest:

2,222,222 i-laanh i-sinx i-waanc i-cin nyeic-baeqv nyic-ziepc

Notice how the Mien i and the Chinese-derived nyeic or its variant nyic complement each other. If there's a gap right before the 'ones', (one to nine) position, then the 'ones' are expressed by the Mien i as in nyeic-baeqv i, '202' (which has a gap at the 'tens' position) as against nyeic-baeqv nyic-ziepc-nyeic, '222' (without such a gap).

Some further combinations are:

1991	yiet-cin juov-baeqv juov-ziepc-yietv uovhnyaangz
555	hmmz-baeqv hmmz-ziepc-hmmz
505	hmmz-baeqv biaa

The Chinese-derived faam, 'three' (used only in certain combinations, as explained above) has the variant faah in faah-ziepc, '30'.

Time Words
Basic time words can also be used as classifiers:

day	hnoi
10 days	ziepc hnoi
month	hlaax

four months	biei hlaax
year	hnyaangx
six years	juqv hnyaangx
yesterday	aah-hnoi
today	ih-hnoi
tomorrow	njang-hnoi
day after tomorrow	hnang-hnoi
this morning	aah ndorm
this evening	aav deix hitv taang lungh maanz

MIEN

OTHER GROUPS

KAREN

Most Karen live in Myanmar (Burma), where there are nearly four million. Three main Karen groups, each speaking a distinct language, also live in smaller numbers along the western border of Thailand. The largest group in Thailand are the Sgaw in the north-west; also substantial are the Pho or Phlong, along the western border south of Chiang Mai. The Kayinni, Red Karen or Kayah are represented by a few villages in extreme north-western Mae Hong Son province; both Pho and Sgaw villages are very widespread in that province. Thai statistics suggest nearly 400,000 Karen, but this is probably an underestimation as many Karen pass as Thai. In Thai there are two words, Yang and Kariang, both of which refer to Karen. Yang is used more in the north and thus often refers to Sgaw, and Kariang is the official name for the group as a whole.

There are major cultural and linguistic differences within the Karen group. The northern subgroups include about half a million Pa-O (Burmese name Taungthu) around Taunggyi in the southern Shan state of Myanmar and over 100,000 Kayan (Burmese name Padaung) and closely related subgroups a bit further south. Female Kayan wear spectacular numbers of neck and leg rings. There are a few Kayan 'long neck' villages in Thailand, and one Pa-o village. The largest of the various central subgroups is the Kayah or Kayinni (Burmese: Red Karen). They are the main nationality in Myanmar's Kayah state, adjacent to northern Mae Hong Son province and number about 300,000. This main central dialect has been studied by David Solnit, who has just published a grammar, *Eastern Kayah Li* (University of Hawaii Press, 1997); others include the Manu, Yintale, Blimaw, Bre (or Keyo) and Geba, totalling some 80,000 people in the west of the Kayah state and the extreme north of the Karen state, Kawthulay.

Karen in Thailand

MYANMAR

Chiang Rai

LAOS

Mae Hong
Song

Phayao

Chiang Mai

Nan

Lamphun

Lampang

Phrae

Uttaradit

Loei

Tak

Sukhotai

Phitsanulok

Phetchabun

Kamphaeng
Phet

Phichit

THAILAND

Nakhon Sawan

Uthai Thani

ANDAMAN
SEA

Suphan Buri

Kanchanaburi

BANGKOK

Ratchaburi

Bight of
Bangkok

Phetchaburi

0   100   200 km

	Pho
	Red
	Sgaw

The two language varieties widely spoken all down Thailand's western border are Sgaw and Pho; they form the southern sub-group of Karen, but are still quite distinct from each other. These two Karen subgroups have probably been in Thailand for nearly 300 years, gradually drifting in from the west. About 1.5 million Sgaw live in Myanmar, partly scattered through the delta regions and partly in the northern Karen state, Kawthulay. A slightly smaller number of Pho live in southern Kawthulay and the delta. Some two-thirds of the Karen in Thailand, more than 250,000 people, are Sgaw, living north of Mae Sariang in Mae Hong Son province, and to the east north of Chiang Mai and Lampang. Most of the rest, and nearly all those south of Mae Sariang or Lamphun, are Pho. There are around 120,000 in Thailand, where they're sometimes known as Phlong, from their word for 'people', just as Sgaw means 'people' in the Sgaw variety of Karen.

The Karen language is historically closer to Burmese and the Tibeto-Burman languages of Thailand including Lahu, Akha and Lisu. However, it's also been influenced by long contacts with Mon-Khmer languages such as Lavüa; and like those languages, as well as Thai, Mong and Mien, it has the verb after the subject noun, rather than at the end of the sentence as in other Tibeto-Burman languages. There's also evidence of cultural convergence, as in the Karen use of drums for religious purposes, also found among many Mon-Khmer groups.

The main authority figure in the Karen village is the priest, sapwa hi ahku (Sgaw) or shasha g'eh ahku (Pho), an elderly man well-versed in Karen traditions. He leads the men in the annual fertility rituals and in the harvest festival. In Karen society female kinship is more important than it is in most other hill tribes; there are also annual sacrifices to the matrilineal ancestor spirit, led by the oldest woman in each kinship group. Other sacrifices are made at various stages in the fields; some field spirits are also female. Apart from these traditional Karen activities, the Christian and Buddhist missionaries have converted large numbers of Karen, and there are various internal Karen religious movements from time to time as well.

OTHER GROUPS

Karen clothing is very attractive, characterised by bright colours, especially reds and whites, in vertical or horizontal stripes. Unmarried girls wear mainly white with a few red stripes (more red among the Pho, especially at the bottom of the dress); married women wear a sarong with narrow horizontal stripes of various colours, mostly red, and a sleeveless shirt with elaborate horizontal patterns in various colours. Men wear sleeveless shirts with vertical stripes, mostly red and white, and much plainer sarongs with horizontal striped patterns. This clothing has been widely copied by Thai clothing manufacturers and is available very cheaply throughout Thailand; but the original is made entirely by hand and is of much better quality and therefore more expensive. Other craftware includes shoulder bags, blankets, beads, earrings, bracelets, pipes and basketry.

Karen houses are mostly rather small, built of bamboo and thatch, high on raised posts and with a covered front porch. The average number of people in a house is also small, with less tendency to have a large extended family in one house; but relatives tend to live nearby. Economic life revolves around the limited number of irrigated rice fields; unlike other hill tribes, many Karen have at least a small area of this much more productive land. In addition there's a controlled and ecologically safe rotation system for unirrigated slash-and-burn agriculture. With population pressure, including a large number of Thais moving in and getting title to traditional Karen land, this system is at risk. Many Karen males also work for wages, in their area or elsewhere in Thailand. Unlike some other hill tribes, the Karen haven't been growing opium, but some Karen are users.

Some important phrases in the standard dialects of Sgaw and Pho from Myanmar follow; there are major dialect differences even within these two varieties, so don't be too surprised if they don't work well in the villages you may visit. Most Karen in Thailand speak Thai quite well, though many have a strong Karen accent, so you may be able to communicate in Thai when necessary.

Sounds
The sounds of Karen and the other languages in this section are indicated approximately, with marks above the vowel to show the tone as usual in Thai:

unmarked	for mid tone
´	for high tone
à	for low tone
^	for falling tone
ˇ	for rising tone

OTHER GROUPS

The usual aspiration contrast is present; aspirated sounds are written with a preceding 'h'. Eu represents a vowel like 'u' or 'o' but with the lips spread rather than rounded; aw is the vowel of English 'awe', e is for the vowel of English 'bait', and eh for the vowel of English 'bet'. An apostrophe after the vowel, ', represents a syllable cut off with a glottal stop, and 'g' is like a French 'r' sound. Both Pho and Sgaw have writing systems derived from Burmese, and Sgaw also has a traditional writing system, not very widely known and sometimes called 'chicken tracks'. A few Karen in Thailand are familiar with one or more of these writing systems, but not enough to make it useful here.

Sgaw Karen
(spoken north of Mae Sariang, Chiang Mai and Lampang)

Are you well?	Ná ô hsû há?
[a usual greeting]	
Yes.	Mè.
What is your name?	Ná mi dà lèh?
My name is ...	Yá mi mè ... law.
Where do you live?	Ná ô hpéh lèh?
I live at ...	Yá ô ... law.
I have come for a visit.	Yá pá héh ha' law.
Eat rice!	Âw me!
Drink hot water!	Áw thí hkyo!
Thank you very much.	Tà byu' dô law.

Pho Karen
(spoken south of Mae Sariang and Lamphun)

Are you well?	Ná àw hsàw hà?
[a usual greeting]	
Yes.	Mwéh.
What is your name?	Ná mîn pá thê lèh?
My name is ...	Yá mîn mwéh ... lâw.
Where do you live?	Ná ò hkò lèh?

I live at ...
I have come for a visit.
Eat rice!
Drink hot water!
Thank you very much.

Yá ò là ... lâw.
Yá pá g'êh g'à' lô hà.
Ân me!
Aw thî hklàn!!
Hsà hkawn hsà ta má' lâw.

MON-KHMER GROUPS

In Nan province there are about 60 villages with over 50,000 people of a group called Htin in some official Thai sources, called Lua by the local Northern Thais, and divided into two subgroups called Mal and Pray (another 15,000 live nearby in Laos). There is no name for the whole group, so these people may sometimes refer to themselves, especially when speaking with Thais, as Lua. A few of this group also live in Laos. The security situation in their area has been problematic for many years, and they are rarely visited. Most also speak Northern Thai.

Also in Nan province, and with a few villages in eastern Chiang Rai, are the Khmu of Thailand, numbering about 8000. These represent a tiny proportion of the total Khmu population, almost all of whom live in northern Laos. There are over 400,000 Khmu in the low hills of north central Laos, about 50,000 in northwestern Vietnam, and a few in China. Some individual Khmu have moved with their work; young men often go to work as samlor (pedicab) drivers in towns, and formerly used to travel long distances to work in the teak extraction trade. As a result there are small Khmu communities in Kanchanaburi province among other places; but these are assimilating into the general Thai population.

More interesting and accessible are the approximately 10,000 Lawa in over 30 villages of south-western Chiang Mai and south-eastern Mae Hong Son provinces. In their own language they call themselves Lavüa. Most of them also speak Northern Thai, but their lifestyle and customs remain somewhat distinct. They live in large villages, mostly near the road between Chiang Mai and Mae Sariang. Local tradition suggests that they were formerly much more widespread and numerous; their language is closely related to those of the Wa, and even more closely to the Palaung (Burmese name), Bulang (Chinese name) or De-ang (own name) and the Benglong. These other groups are very numerous in Myanmar and China, with a couple of stray outlying villages in remote locations in Thailand.

The Mon-Khmer group Palong is found in a few villages to the west of Mae Rim in Chiang Mai province; of some 500 people, only a few still speak the language. This group shouldn't be confused with the much larger group, the Palaung, Bulang or De-ang, of the northern Shan state of Myanmar and extending into China. One village of 'Khamet' is found just north of Wiang Pa Pao on the main road between Chiang Mai and Chiang Rai; these people are Lamet from north-western Laos, and speak a language closely related to Khmu. There are likewise some individual small villages where other languages such as Wa, Mok (known in Chinese as Benglong) and closely related languages are still spoken. Almost all these people are now more comfortable with Northern Thai than their traditional languages, so phrases in their languages are hardly needed.

OTHER HILL TRIBES

There are many other smaller groups in northern and western Thailand which the Thais group under the general term Lawa or in Northern Thai Lua (also used in referring to the Htin and Lavüa). Most of these are more extensively influenced by Thai culture than the groups discussed above; nearly all also speak some variety of Thai. This category includes three groups whose languages are more closely related to Lahu, Akha and Lisu: Bisu, Mpi and Gong. There are also several groups which speak languages of the Mon-Khmer family closely related to Lavüa, including Palong, Lamet and others. In almost all cases their culture has effectively disappeared and their languages are gradually dying. These groups are all Buddhist and have adopted rural Thai lifestyle.

Other Hill Tribes in Thailand

MYANMAR

LAOS

Chiang Rai

Mae Hong Song

Phayao

Chiang Mai

Nan

Lamphun

Lampang

Phrae

Uttaradit

Loei

Tak

Sukhotai

Phitsanulok

Kamphaeng Phet

Phichit

Phetchabun

THAILAND

Nakhon Sawan

Uthai Thani

ANDAMAN SEA

Suphan Buri

Kanchanaburi

BANGKOK

Ratchaburi

Bight of Bangkok

Phetchaburi

0   100   200 km

OTHER GROUPS

	Htin
	Khmu
	Gong (3)
	Bisu (3)
	Phalong (2)
	Lavüa (32)
	Mpi (1)

Gong

The Gong used to be a much more widespread group, with many other villages in Kanchanaburi province and extending eastwards into the fringes of the central plain; these have now become Thai or, in a few cases, Karen villages. Quite distinct dialects are spoken in the two surviving villages; here are a few phrases in the dialect of Kok Chiang village in Dan Chang district, Suphanburi province. The Gong villages are fairly near to rarely visited Pho Karen villages. If you use some of the following phrases, the villagers will be pleased to hear you using their language.

Where are you going?	(Nàwng) a náwng kàwwê?
I have come to visit.	(Ngá) kawíng di-o.
What is your name?	Nàwng hong nyéung a hkéng yang wê?
My name is ...	Ngá nyéung ...
Have you eaten?	Mang sa lá?
I have eaten.	Mang sí hke.
Thank you. (lit: very good)	Ang kêun.
Where is the Karen village?	Kaleng hpyé a htô wê?

Bisu

The Bisu are closely related to several other small groups including the 30,000 Phunoi of north-eastern Laos, the Cong of Vietnam, and the Pyen of Myanmar. They're also found in China, where they're called Laomian. It's likely that they were brought as war captives from the north by the rulers of Chiang Rai during the 19th century. There are also some former Bisu villages elsewhere in Chiang Rai and Phayao provinces, where the oldest people can still remember a bit of the language. The most vigorous is the dialect of Huai Chomphu (Pink Stream) village; this is near the foot of Doi Chang south-west of Chiang Rai, and only a short detour south from the path to Lisu and Akha villages there. Here are some phrases in this dialect.

Where are you going?	(Nang) lakéung é-éu.
I am coming for a visit.	(Ga) leu-ngé.
What is your name?	Nang ang hméng ma cheu?
My name is ...	Ga hméng ...
Have you eaten?	Hàng tsà là?
I have eaten.	Hàng tsà-keu.
Thank you. (lit: very good)	Ang hmèn yá.
Where is the path to the Lisu village?	Lisu hkàwng kíbà lakéung é-éu?

Mpi

The Mpi have a traditional tale that they were brought as war captives before 1800 from Sipsongphanna in what is now China; indeed, their language is very similar to Piyo and Hkatu, which are still spoken there. (In Chinese, Biyue and Kaduo; according to the Chinese classification these are 'dialects' spoken by subgroups of the Hani nationality which also includes Akha.) All Mpi speak Northern Thai; younger people also speak standard Thai, learned in the village school; but most villagers still speak their own language too, and are proud of it. The local Northern Thais call them Kaw, which has sometimes led officials to confuse them with the Akha (in Thai; Ikaw).

Where are you going?	Na hà yé?
I am going for a visit.	Ngó só í he.
What is your name?	Nà m mí n ché á?
My name is ...	Nga m mí ...
Have you eaten?	(Na) hà chò là?
I have eaten.	(Ngó) hà chò so.
Thank you. (lit: very good)	Mèu mèu.

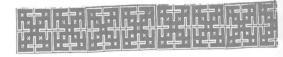

INDEX

TEXT

MONG 99

MUHSO .... (see Lahu)

MUSUR .... (see Lahu)

MYAUNG .... (see Mong)

NOTES

NOTES

NOTES

NOTES

LONELY PLANET PHRASEBOOKS

Complete your travel experience with a Lonely Planet phrasebook. Developed for the independent traveller, the phrasebooks enable you to communicate confidently in any practical situation – and get to know the local people and their culture.

Skipping lengthy details on where to get your drycleaning ironed, information in the phrasebooks covers bargaining, customs and protocol, how to address people and introduce yourself, explanations of local ways of telling the time, dealing with bureaucracy and bargaining, plus plenty of ways to share your interests and learn from locals.

Arabic (Egyptian)
Arabic (Moroccan)
Australian
  *Introduction to Australian English,
  Aboriginal and Torres Strait languages*
Baltic States
  *Covers Estonian, Latvian and
  Lithuanian*
Bengali
Brazilian
Burmese
Cantonese
Central Asia
Central Europe
  *Covers Czech, French, German,
  Hungarian, Italian and Slovak*
Eastern Europe
  *Covers Bulgarian, Czech, Hungarian,
  Polish, Romanian and Slovak.*
Ethiopian (Amharic)
Fijian
French
German
Greek
Hindi/Urdu
Indonesian
Italian
Japanese
Korean
Lao
Malay
Mandarin
Mediterranean Europe
  *Covers Albanian, Croatian, Greek,
  Italian, Macedonian, Maltese, Serbian
  and Slovene*

Mongolian
Nepali
Papua New Guinea (Pidgin)
Pilipino (Tagalog)
Quechua
Russian
Scandinavian Europe
  *Covers Danish, Finnish, Icelandic,
  Norwegian and Swedish*
South-East Asia
  *Covers Burmese, Indonesian, Khmer,
  Lao, Malay, Tagalog (Pilipino), Thai and
  Vietnamese*
Spanish (Castilian)
  *Also includes Basque, Catalan andGali-
  cian*
Spanish (Latin American)
Sri Lanka
Swahili
Thai
Thai Hill Tribes
Tibetan
Turkish
Ukrainian
USA
  *Introduction to US English,
  Vernacular, Native American
  languages and Hawaiian*
Vietnamese
Western Europe
  *Useful words and phrases in Basque,
  Catalan, Dutch, French, German,
  Greek, Irish, Italian, Portuguese,
  Scottish Gaelic, Spanish (Castilian) and
  Welsh*

COMPLETE LIST OF LONELY PLANET BOOKS

AFRICA
Africa - the South • Africa on a shoestring • Arabic (Moroccan) phrasebook • Cairo • Cape Town • Central Africa • East Africa • Egypt • Egypt travel atlas • Ethiopian (Amharic) phrasebook • The Gambia & Sengal • Kenya • Kenya travel atlas • Malawi, Mozambique & Zambia • Morocco • North Africa • South Africa, Lesotho & Swaziland • South Africa, Lesotho & Swaziland travel atlas • Swahili phrasebook • Tunisia • Trekking in East Africa • West Africa • Zimbabwe, Botswana & Namibia • Zimbabwe, Botswana & Namibia travel atlas
Travel Literature: The Rainbird: A Central African Journey • Songs to an African Sunset: A Zimbabwean Story

ANTARCTICA
Antarctica

AUSTRALIA & THE PACIFIC
Australia • Australian phrasebook • Bushwalking in Australia • Bushwalking in Papua New Guinea • Fiji • Fijian phrasebook • Islands of Australia's Great Barrier Reef • Melbourne • Micronesia • New Caledonia • New South Wales • New Zealand • Northern Territory • Outback Australia • Papua New Guinea • Papua New Guinea phrasebook • Queensland • Rarotonga & the Cook Islands • Samoa • Solomon Islands • South Australia • Sydney • Tahiti & French Polynesia • Tasmania • Tonga • Tramping in New Zealand • Vanuatu • Victoria • Western Australia
Travel Literature: Islands in the Clouds • Sean & David's Long Drive

CENTRAL AMERICA & THE CARIBBEAN
Bahamas, Turks & Caicos • Bermuda • Central America on a shoestring • Costa Rica • Cuba • Eastern Caribbean • Guatemala, Belize & Yucatán: La Ruta Maya • Jamaica
Travel Literature: Green Dreams: Travels in Central America

EUROPE
Amsterdam • Andalucia • Austria • Baltics States phrasebook • Berlin • Britain • Canary Islands • Central Europe on a shoestring • Central Europe phrasebook • Czech & Slovak Republics • Denmark • Dublin • Eastern Europe on a shoestring • Eastern Europe phrasebook • Estonia, Latvia & Lithuania • Finland • France • French phrasebook • Germany • German phrasebook • Greece • Greek phrasebook • Hungary • Iceland, Greenland & the Faroe Islands • Ireland • Italian phrasebook • Italy • Lisbon • London • Mediterranean Europe on a shoestring • Mediterranean Europe phrasebook • Paris • Poland • Portugal • Portugal travel atlas • Prague • Romania & Moldova • Russia, Ukraine & Belarus • Russian phrasebook • Scandinavian & Baltic Europe on a shoestring • Scandinavian Europe phrasebook • Slovenia • Spain • Spanish phrasebook • St Petersburg • Switzerland • Trekking in Spain • Ukrainian phrasebook • Vienna • Walking in Britain • Walking in Italy • Walking in Switzerland • Western Europe on a shoestring • Western Europe phrasebook
Travel Literature: The Olive Grove: Travels in Greece

INDIAN SUBCONTINENT
Bangladesh • Bengali phrasebook • Bhutan • Delhi • Goa • Hindi/Urdu phrasebook • India • India & Bangladesh travel atlas • Indian Himalaya • Karakoram Highway • Nepal • Nepali phrasebook • Pakistan • Rajasthan • Sri Lanka • Sri Lanka phrasebook • Trekking in the Indian Himalaya • Trekking in the Karakoram & Hindukush • Trekking in the Nepal Himalaya
Travel Literature: In Rajasthan • Shopping for Buddhas

COMPLETE LIST OF LONELY PLANET BOOKS

ISLANDS OF THE INDIAN OCEAN
Madagascar & Comoros • Maldives • Mauritius, Réunion & Seychelles

NORTH AMERICA
Alaska • Backpacking in Alaska • Baja California • California & Nevada • Canada • Chicago• Deep South • Florida • Hawaii • Honolulu • Los Angeles • Mexico • Mexico City • Miami • New England • New Orleans • New York City • New York, New Jersey & Pennsylvania • Pacific Northwest USA • Rocky Mountain States • San Francisco • Seattle • South-West China • Southwest USA • USA phrasebook • Washington, DC & the Capital Region
Travel Literature: Drive thru America

NORTH-EAST ASIA
Beijing • Cantonese phrasebook • China • Hong Kong • Hong Kong, Macau & Guangzhou • Japan • Japanese phrasebook • Japanese audio pack • Korea • Korean phrasebook • Mandarin phrasebook • Mongolia • Mongolian phrasebook • North-East Asia on a shoestring • Seoul • Taiwan • Tibet • Tibet phrasebook • Tokyo
Travel Literature: Lost Japan

MIDDLE EAST & CENTRAL ASIA
Arab Gulf States • Arabic (Egyptian) phrasebook • Cairo • Central Asia • Central Asia phrasebook • Iran • Israel & the Palestinian Territories • Israel & the Palestinian Territories travel atlas • Istanbul • Jerusalem • Jordan & Syria • Jordan, Syria & Lebanon travel atlas • Lebanon • Middle East • Turkey • Turkish phrasebook • Turkey travel atlas • Yemen
Travel Literature: The Gates of Damascus • Kingdom of the Film Stars: Journey into Jordan

SOUTH AMERICA
Argentina, Uruguay & Paraguay • Bolivia • Brazil • Brazilian phrasebook • Buenos Aires • Chile & Easter Island • Chile & Easter Island travel atlas • Colombia • Ecuador & the Galápagos Islands • Latin American Spanish phrasebook • Peru • Quechua phrasebook • Rio de Janeiro • South America on a shoestring • Trekking in the Patagonian Andes • Venezuela
Travel Literature: Full Circle: A South American Journey

SOUTH-EAST ASIA
Bali & Lombok • Bangkok • Burmese phrasebook• Cambodia • Ho Chi Minh City • Indonesia • Indonesian phrasebook • Indonesian audio pack • Jakarta • Java • Laos • Laos travel atlas • Lao phrasebook • Malay phrasebook • Malaysia, Singapore & Brunei • Myanmar (Burma) • Philippines • Pilipino phrasebook • Singapore• South-East Asia on a shoestring • South-East Asia phrasebook • Thailand • Thailand's Islands & Beaches • Thailand travel atlas • Thai phrasebook • Thai Hill Tribes phrasebook • Thai audio pack • Vietnam • Vietnamese phrasebook • Vietnam travel atlas

ALSO AVAILABLE: Brief Encounters • Not the Only Planet• Travel with Children •Traveller's Tales

For ordering information contact your nearest Lonely Planet office.

PLANET TALK

Lonely Planet's FREE quarterly newsletter

Every issue is packed with up-to-date travel news
and advice including:

* a letter from Lonely Planet co-founders Tony and
  Maureen Wheeler
* go behind the scenes on the road with a Lonely
  Planet author
* feature article on an important and topical travel
  issue
* a selection of recent letters from travellers
* details on forthcoming Lonely Planet promotions
* complete list of Lonely Planet products

To join our mailing list contact any Lonely Planet office.

LONELY PLANET PUBLICATIONS

AUSTRALIA
PO Box 617, Hawthorn 3122, Victoria
tel: (03) 9819 1877 fax: (03) 9819 6459
e-mail: talk2us@lonelyplanet.com.au

USA
150 Linden Street,
Oakland, CA 94607
tel: (510) 893 8555
TOLL FREE: 800 275-8555
fax: (510) 893 8572
e-mail: info@lonelyplanet.com

UK
10a Spring Place,
London NW5 3BH
tel: (0171) 428 2800 fax: (0171) 428 4828
e-mail: go@lonelyplanet.co.uk

FRANCE:
1 rue du Dahomey, 75011 Paris, France
tel: 01 55 25 33 00 fax: 01 55 25 33 01
e-mail: bip@lonelyplanet.fr

World Wide Web: http://www.lonelyplanet.com
or AOL keyword: lp